Work In Retirement

The Persistence of an American Collective Representation

Fatemeh Givechian

UNIVERSITY
PRESS OF
AMERICA

Lanham • New York • London

Copyright © 1990 by
University Press of America®, Inc.
4720 Boston Way
Lanham, Maryland 20706

3 Henrietta Street
London WC2E 8LU England

Library of Congress Cataloging-in-Publication Data

Givechian, Fatemeh, 1953—
Work in retirement: the persistence of an American collective
representation / Fatemeh Givechian.
p. cm.
Includes bibliographical references (p.   ) and index.
1. Work ethic — United States. 2. Aged — United States — Societies
and clubs.   I. Title.
HD8072.5.G58   1990
306.3'613'0846 — dc20   90-12713 CIP
ISBN 0-8191-7852-7 (alk. paper)
ISBN 0-8191-7853-5 (pbk.: alk. paper)

 The paper used in this publication meets the minimum requirements of
American National Standard for Information Sciences—Permanence
of Paper for Printed Library Materials, ANSI Z39.48–1984.

To SAEID BAHMANY
A Family Friend for All Seasons

TABLE OF CONTENTS

Preface and Acknowledgements

This study investigates the notion of "work" as a cultural category in the United States through the study of senior citizens, a stratum of the population who have progressed beyond the work stage. Conducted primarily at a Senior Citizen Center membering over 1100 persons over the age of 55, the research is both diachronic and synchronic. The former consists of library research and the study of the Senior Center archives in its 25 year history. The latter mainly consists of participant observation in all the activities offered by the Center, as well as interviewing the elderly.

While existing studies of Senior Centers portray the function of these activity centers as social and recreational, this study argues that the cultural significance of these centers lies in their function as a substitute for work. The more the activities resemble work, the more they are welcomed by the members. Thus, there is a metaphoric relationship between senior citizens and workers, and between Senior Centers and work places. By taking roles found in work places such as president and vice-president, while implementing organized activities, the elderly re-become the kind of differentiated individuals they once were in the work sphere. The elderly introduce elements of work (hierarchy, assembly lines, reward) into their activities. The study leads to the conclusion that the metaphoric relationship between the activities in the work sphere and those of the elderly in activity centers helps the elderly to regenerate "self-identity."

The present book is a revised version of a doctoral dissertation whose fieldwork was done during 1983-1986. I owe Professor H. L. Seneviratne more than I can put into words. Not only did he help me academically, spending endless hours to discuss various parts, he combined them with emotional support and friendship. Professors Ravindra S. Khare, David J. Sapir, and Murray Milner, deserve many thanks for their reading of this manuscript as a dissertation. I am also grateful to my professors and colleagues Roy Wagner, Susan McKinnon, Peter Metcalf, Fredrick Damon, Christopher Crocker, Charles Kaut, Steven Ploy, Marion Ross, and Carrie Douglass who either read earlier drafts of this work or were helpful to me during my graduate studies. Special mention should be made of late Professors Victor Turner and Edwin Erickson, who encouraged me a great deal but never saw the finished product. A word of thanks to the anonymous reader(s) who read the manuscript for the publisher and made insightful comments.

I owe a great deal to those who in one way or another facilitated my fieldwork. Each in their official or unofficial capacity were invaluable to the work. For the purpose of anonymity I do not write their titles, but just their names. Ms. Elizabeth Seabrook, Mrs. Ruth Depiro, Ms. Dottie Webber, Mrs. Nancy Damon, and Ms. Ashlena Manson were of enormous help. Mr. Robert Damon and his wife, Grace, sheltered me in their home when I carried out fieldwork in a Southern State, while Mr. Fred Wilcox and his wife, LaVergne, helped me with the fieldwork in a Northern State. Thanks are due to the many individuals, whom I was never fortunate to meet, who sent me brochures, schedules and other information from various Senior Centers across the country. I owe more, however, to the many senior citizens who made me, the intruder anthropologist, feel welcome. The work is more theirs than mine. Finally, I would like to thank M. R. Ghanoonparvar, his wife Diane Wilcox, "my second family," who have helped me always, and facilitated the final printing of this manuscript. The use of computer facilities at the University of Arizona for the proccessing of the manuscript is hereby gratefully acknowledged.

Last, but not least, I owe a great deal to my husband, Dr. Farhang Rajaee, and my daughters, Bita Mehrin, Azadeh Nikoo and Farzaneh Sheyda. Farhang not only helped me take care of the children, but read various drafts and revised versions of the work and provided me with valuable comments.

Fatemeh Givechian (Rajaee)
Tehran, February 1990

2

Chapter I

Preliminary Discussions

It is 2:45 on a Wednesday afternoon in the autumn. It is cold and rainy outside. The place is the Senior Citizen Center, in a medium sized town, where a variety of activities are offered for the senior citizens. 3:00 to 4:00 p.m. on Wednesdays is set for the "rhythm band." Senior citizens are arriving gradually. Two of them walk with canes in hand. The elderly greet one another and, while picking a musical instrument out of a bag, sit on the chairs they usually consider theirs. Those who play similar instruments sit next to one another. A few minutes before 3:00, a middle aged woman arrives and sits at the piano. She smiles constantly and is very friendly to everybody. Around 3:00, a young woman in her late thirties arrives. She also greets everybody, asks how each person is doing and whether he/she feels better.[1] She is the conductor of the band. The piano player and the conductor are professional musicians and are not members of the Senior Center. They go to the Center to voluntarily help the senior citizens to "play" the music. It is a little past 3:00 o'clock now. The piano player is ready to play. The conductor is facing the two rows of senior citizens (usually twelve persons) who are each displaying the gesture of readyness to play a musical instrument: a drum, a set of bells, shakes, tambourines, triangles, and sticks. I, the anthropologist doing fieldwork, am also sitting among the players and given a shake to play. The piano player and the conductor are the only ones who know how to read music. Others do not know music and do not have any "note sheets" in front of them. They watch the conductor and

3

play their musical instruments according to her commands. When the conductor wants someone to play she points to that person and shows with her fingers how many times he/she should hit or shake the instrument. Although the news about the rhythm band has been publically announced in the monthly newsletter of the Center, there is no audience in the room to listen to the music. Except for the sound of the piano and the set of bells, other instruments do not produce a pleasant sound to me. Actually, it often seems that the sound combination of other instruments ruins the beauty of the sounds of the piano and the set of bells.

The rhythm band plays about ten different songs most of which have been "hits" during the 1920s and 1930s. At 4:00 o'clock the elderly stop in accordance with the set program and terminate their "activity." Placing their musical instruments in the bag, they get ready to leave. Edith and Pasha go to the phone and call for taxis. Leidia and George live in nearby towns 20 and 35 miles far from here respectively. Arthur has to walk to the bank where his daughter works, and wait there for 45 minutes until she gets off work to give him a ride home. Hazel who is 90 years old, the oldest member of the rhythm band, although lives close to the Center, tells me that it takes her "20 minutes to walk home." I ask her whether she still wants to walk in the rain and cold weather. She says: "I don't like cold weather, but I have warm clothes on. I also have my umbrella. I don't enjoy walking on such a rainy day, but it is cheaper this way." I offer to give her a ride. She is reluctant, but realizing my sincerity, she accepts the offer. In the car, Hazel and I talk about various things. I ask her whether she enjoys going to the Senior Center. She replies: "Yes." I ask her "even on such a day?" Thinking for a moment, she smiles and says: "Well, I think I should go. I have been a member of the rhythm band for thirteen years."

After taking Hazel home safely, driving in the rain, I think about what I have seen today. By now, I have been doing fieldwork at the Senior Center for five months. Since I knew English, the language of my informants, before going to the field, I could communicate easily from the first day. As a foreign born studying in the United States, I was constantly comparing the elderly at the Center and what they did with the elderly in my own homeland. Today I thought my old fellowcountrymen would probably never come out on such a day, or even on a sunny day, to do "hits and shakes" only. They would probably find it "strange" or even "pointless." Considering their expected cultural role, perhaps they would be too busy to have time for such things. Such a comparison, while inevitable, bothered me somewhat and made me angry with myself. I hated to be biased. "I was studying anthropology. I shouldn't have thought this way. I should have been more universal-minded and aware of cultural diversities," I reminded myself. But I couldn't stop seeing the American elderly with my "outsider's eyes." I remembered my grandparents and other elderly whom I knew, and those whom my friends and acquaintances knew. They wouldn't behave like that, I was sure. I reminded myself of the lesson I was taught in the school I was studying: "An anthropologist must learn the reason behind the native's behavior." I asked myself: What was the reason behind these people's behavior? Was there any reason at all? Why did the senior citizens get out of the house on such a cold rainy day to go to the Senior Center? Why did they make the sacrifice of paying for the taxi, driving thirty miles, or walking in the rain? Except for a few minutes of greeting and a few minutes of conversation before leaving, no fellowship took place. Senior citizens did not make anything tangible (e.g., a crafted object) to take home and use it. They did not learn any music either, they just "shook and hit" their musical instruments. I have been with the rhythm band every Wednesday afternoon. The elderly come for a particular activity, do what is assigned (in this case, playing the music), and then leave. But why? This is the central question of this book.

As a student of American culture, my first lesson was the realization of the significance of the "individual" in American ideology. Before starting the fieldwork, my original concern was to examine the interaction between the individual and society. In other words, I wanted to understand the status and the place of an "individual" in the society. But my bafflement with the behavior of the elderly in the Center shifted my focus somewhat. I had always admired American people's hard work which in turn contributed to the making of a successful industrial society. But the elderly's absorption in work related mores and pattern of behavior was puzzling. It appeared as though they defined and identified themselves in terms of what they did or with regard to their membership to various organizations. In short, what they do and the way in which they do it gives the impression that they "work."

Hence, this book will focus on the notion of "work" as a cultural category in the United States through the study of the activities of senior citizens,[2] a stratum of people who have progressed beyond the work stage. There is consensus among students of American culture concerning the key concepts constituting what might be called American ideology. Equality, anti-authoritarianism, individual's self-reliance and independence, a sense of efficiency, innovativeness and openness to new experience comprise the main features of American ideology (De Tocqueville 1835; Vogt 1958; Barnett and Silverman 1978; Inkeles 1980). If one were to identify a central notion encompassing all of these, the notion of "work" would stand out as the most appropriate. It is through work that one achieves self-reliance and independence, efficiency, innovativeness, etc.

Scholarly recognition of "work" and the "work ethic" in an industrial society in general, and in American culture in particular has a rather long history (Weber 1958; De Tocqueville 1835; Dahl 1972; O'Toole *et al.* 1978). Several studies report that when Americans are given a chance to put their own personal failures to bad health, accidents, luck or God's will, they actually deny the importance of these factors (Morgan et al. 1964; Strumpel 1976). Rather, they attribute failure to their own inability to exercise certain virtues, the most widely cited being hard work, persistence, and taking initiative (Morgan et al. 1964; Inkeles 1980). Back in 1830s, De Tocqueville observed the tendency to attribute the improvement or decline in one's economic conditions to one's own effort and accomplishments as a distinctive American characteristic. He acknowledged that Americans "are apt to imagine that their whole destiny is in their own hands" (De Tocqueville 1835:44). Americans attest to the importance of achievement through one's effort by their desire to read "success stories"; the stories of those who present the "rags to riches" or the "log-cabin to the White House" ideal (Warner 1953).

A. Three Age Grades in American Society

Among attitudes to work of the three age-grades - children, adults, and the elderly - that of the elderly is the most ambiguous and paradoxical one. The younger generation, which is preparing itself to enter the work sphere, epitomizes the attitude of "pre-work."

Adults are actually involved in the work sphere. The elderly who are outside that sphere represent a "post-work" attitude which, one would suppose, might be a "retirement attitude." In fact, in American culture the elderly value work as much as other age-grades. Owing to their old age, however, they are expelled from the work sphere. Hence the ambiguity and paradox.

In most societies, the norm of the activities for the three age-grades (children, adults, the elderly) is that children are trained for adulthood, adults work and prepare for the well-being of both children and old people, and the elderly either do not retire at all (Hughes 1961), or retire but resume spiritual (Rustom 1961) or ritualistic and family related functions (Smith 1961). Although it is hard to generalize, in the United States, the lives of children and adults resemble those of other societies. The case of the elderly is somewhat different. Generally speaking, there is an abrupt retirement from work for most people. In many cases, a special ritual called the retirement party, signifies the exclusion of the retiree from the work sphere. Formally, the retiree should withdraw from the "work" sphere and accept a complacent life in the "home" sphere.

Reality tells a different story. There are many institutions in the United States that offer organized activities for the elderly. The elderly have the choice of (or the need for?) getting together and involving themselves in those activities. In other words, a new phase of "working" in an organized manner is created for them. It appears that retirement is only metaphorically synonymous with leisure and rest. Retirees seem to treat retirement as entering a new phase of the work sphere by occupying themselves with systematic activities offered by various organizations.

The paradox and ambiguity between formal retirement and involvement in work as a value-orientation makes the American elderly a fruitful group for the study of American culture. Such a study, moreover, would help a better understanding of the spheres of work and home in the United States. Do the activities of retirees resemble the activities performed at work or home? My field research in a Senior Citizen Center has revealed that not only are those activities presented to the elderly as work, but the elderly themselves treat them as work. One can even summarize their behavior as "playing work." By the usage of the term "play," I have in mind children's play such as playing barbers, tea parties, teachers, etc., in which the players assume the roles of barber/customer, host/guest, teacher/student, etc. I use the phrase "playing work" for senior citizens meaning that when senior citizens take part in various kinds of activities (e.g., crafting, travelling, playing games and cards, educational classes), they perform them as if they were working in the work sphere. They take on the roles of the work sphere such as president, vice-president, treasurer, and secretary, and introduce various elements of work, (e.g. fixed time, assembly line, competition, achievement, reward ("salary")).

In their study of Senior Citizen Centers, Hanssen *et al.* (1978: 193-199) and Krout (1983: 339-352) suggest that these Centers function primarily as social and recreational settings. They do not examine the nature, meaning and consequence of those social functions. While I agree that Senior Centers have been set up to offer variety of recreational and social activities, I believe that their cultural significance and primary contribution lie in their function as a substitute for work; they are imitations of work places. The more the activities resemble work the more they are welcomed by members. Thus, there is a metaphoric relationship between senior citizens and workers, and between Senior Centers and work places (senior citizens: Senior Centers:: workers: work places). (See Levi-Strauss 1962, 1963; Sapir and Crocker 1977).

I am not suggesting that the Senior Centers are merely work places or their imitations. Rather, I argue that taking them as recreational places in the conventional sense does not accurately describe them. The forms and the contents of their activities are modeled and performed respectively based on the norms and practices of the work place. In other words, the norms, ethos, patterns of behavior, and mores which the sphere of work and work place entail are so pervasive in the society that to an outside observer, the ways in which the elderly spend their time, and function in an activity in the Center resemble work.

B. Theoretical Framework and Method

To present the metaphoric relationship between the Senior Center and work place, I will focus mostly on the activities offered at one Senior Center and the way in which they are performed by members. The findings lead to the general observation that in an industrial society where work is a significant part of the people's lives, retirement, for the members of the culture, means changing the type of work and/or "playing work" rather than withdrawing from work. Studying the attitude of American senior citizens towards work and retirement is extremely important for the following reason. Americans today are living longer and healthier lives compared to their fellow countrymen in 1900s or even 1950s. As Margaret Clark points out:

> For the first time in the history of mankind there exist in large numbers men and women already aged by established chronological standards who can anticipate another full decade or more of life. Industrial society has created a new group (1975:78-88).

Demographic statistics show that in 1830 only one American in twenty-five was sixty years of age or older; in 1960, one out of eight. The number of those over the age of eighty-five has increased more than tenfold since 1920 (ibid.). The population of those over sixty-five was less than five million in 1900. It rose to over twenty million in 1980 (Belsky 1984:5). American senior citizens today are pioneers in the sense that they are the first generation who are, as a group, experiencing such longevity. Considering that mandatory retirement in most professions is between the ages of sixty and sixty-five and many people live up to their nineties, the elderly may have decades of life ahead of them after retirement. The American culture has yet to find ways of incorporating the elderly within the ongoing societal system. The present study is an effort to explore some aspects of these pioneers' culture within the broader American culture as a whole.

Theoretically, this study will mainly draw from symbolic anthropology. By "symbol," I follow David Schneider's definition of that term: "symbol means something which stands for something else, or some things else, where there is no necessary or intrinsic relationship between the symbol and that which it symbolizes" (Schneider 1968:1). I will take into consideration both the role of "ideology" (e.g., the cultural values placed on the independence of the individuals and on success), and purely "external pressures" on individuals (e.g., mandatory retirement). I will also make use of historical materials in order to place the data in a larger framework. Thus, I will stress the continuing process of change in the society, and incorporate the analyses of historical transformations, (e.g., separation of work from home in the first half of the 19th century United States (Johnson 1978; Wallace 1980; Mathaei 1982), and the appearance of mandatory retirement at a fixed age in the late 18th century and its common acceptance in the late 19th century (Fischer 1977:135)).

As the point of departure, I will look for the elderly's purpose in going to activity centers after retirement. This book will show that the elderly are concerned with self-identity, and work is one way in which they define their self-identity. In other words, through organized activities, the elderly create something which may be termed as "self-identity" in order to re-become the kind of "differentiated" individuals they once were in work places.

I will also draw from anthropological studies on work and on old people in various societies, and from gerontological studies on the activities of the elderly in the United States. Anthropological study of old age is a relatively recent phenomenon. For a long time, old people served as informants or as a peripheral topic in anthroplogical studies (e.g., Monica Wilson 1951). Anthropologists did not focus specifically on old age. The ancestral model for cross-cultural studies of old age is Leo Simmons's 1945 book entitled **The Role of the Aged in Primitive Society** which inaugurated a phase in the studies of the elderly and their status and roles. Recently, old people have become the subject of broader "ethnographic" research. The term "ethnography" is used intentionally because the anthropology of old age is essentially an ethnographic enterprise (e.g., S.F. Moore 1978; S. Johnson 1971). Relevant anthropological studies have helped the present research in terms of cross-cultural analysis, and in particular in focusing on the difference between the activities of old people in the United States and those of other societies. These studies may not be of much help theoretically, for as Jennie Keith points out: "Observation and analysis [in the anthropological literature on aging] have been mainly oriented to **gerontological** rather than anthropological theory" (1980:339-364, emphasis added).

Gerontological studies are emphatically based on sociological and psychological theories. These are concerned with patterns of behavior or psychological aspects of old age including the activities of the retirees. They cover many aspects of old age, namely, the elderly's status and roles, family relationships, work and retirement, health and dying, etc. Gerontological studies approach the activities of retired older people from various theoretical angles. Some of the most influential and controversial theories are: disengagement theory, activity theory, functional theory, and continuity theory.

The disengagement theory, first propounded by Cumming and Henry (1961), assumes an inevitable and universal process of mutual withdrawal of the aging individual and society, beneficial to both parties. This theory has been extensively criticized, especially with regard to the claim of universality and inevitability (Atchley 1971). In contrast to disengagement, the activity theory assumes that in order to adjust successfully in retirement to the loss of one's job, one must find a substitute for whatever personal goals the job was used to achieve (Atchley 1976). The activity theory postulates that successful and contented aging depends on the older individual's integration in society, on the contribution he continues to make, and on his feeling of being still useful and needed (Rhee 1974). Unlike the disengagement theoreticians, proponents of activity theory have not made extravagant claims. The theory has consequently not provoked a great deal of critical reaction.

Other theories are consistent with either disengagement or activity theory. For example, the functional theory (consistent with the disengagement theory) directs attention to the "needs" of society which are served by the institution of retirement (Breen 1963). The theory is based on the assumption that society itself has needs apart from those of the individuals and groups which compose it. M.H. Huyck (1974) argues that retirement serves a useful social function in an era when "labor supply exceeds demand," and that retirement eliminates the need to retain workers whose knowledge and skills may be "outdated." The continuity theory (consistent with the activity theory), on the other hand, assumes that, whenever possible, the individual will cope with retirement by increasing the time he spends in roles he already plays rather than by finding new roles to play (Atchley 1976). This theory is based on two assumptions: old people tend to stick with tried patterns of behavior rather than to experiment, and most people want their life in retirement to be as much like their previous life as possible.

Taken in totality, gerontological studies provide many insights into retirement. Nevertheless, they suffer from some problems. They are more theories of optimal aging than activities of retired older people (particularly the activity theory). They are also sociological in the sense that they support the "needs" of the society and economy rather than the needs of the individuals (particularly disengagement and functional theories). Moreover, as Stanly Parker (1982:60) suggests these theories neglect the "meaning of activity in later life." The present study tries to overcome the above-mentioned problems. It tries to deal with the actual activities of retirees rather than optimal ones, it takes into consideration the needs of the individual, and it analyzes the (symbolic) meaning of those activities to the individual. Furthermore, the present study is designed to address specific themes, namely, the understanding of work among the elderly in American culture, and in particular, in that aspect of American culture revealed through the work/home dichotomy. This study explores this dichotomy by the use of insights provided in symbolic analyses (Schneider 1980; Barnett and Silverman 1979; Marx 1973, 1977; Levi-Strauss 1962, 1963; Sapir and Crocker 1977).

In the pursuit of this study, I have done fieldwork mainly in a Senior Citizen Center, one of over 5,000 Senior Centers in the United States (Krout, 1983:339-359), and one of the 170 Senior Centers in its State. The Center is located in a medium-sized historical town in South East United States. The town is a retirement community. Many senior citizens have worked in other places and decided to retire in this town. Located in this town are several Government subsidized housings for the elderly, several nursing homes, several retirement homes, a retirement village, one Adult Day Care Center, an Area Board for Aging, and one Senior Center. In spite of all these facilities for the elderly, the town has not yet become an age-segregated place similar to some cities in Arizona, California, or Florida, where the proportion of the elderly is higher than other age-grades. This was the main reason which attracted me to this community: whereas I was looking for a retirement town, I did not want it to be an age-segregated place.

I first contacted the director of the Senior Center in June 1983, and began regular visits starting July 1983. The data I obtained and the methodology I utilized to collect them can be described as follows:

1.Diachronic study

Studying a society such as the Senior Citizen Center, located in a large-scale industrial society, is very different from a traditional anthropological study of a small tribe, or a village. Traditional diachronic studies are primarily conducted by "reconstructing" the history of the village, clan, tribe, etc., through interviewing older informants. At the Senior Center the members are transient. They join the Center for a certain time; they move out, terminate the membership, or die. Moreover, although some members may be spouses, sisters, or brothers, generally speaking, this is not a kinship based society. Thus, it is unlikely that the members know enough about the Center or about other members to let the anthropologist "reconstruct" the history of the Center and its members. Fortunately, this problem could be resolved by both library research and the study of the Center archives. Library research provided the basic framework for the study of a society like the Senior Center. It also provided general information on retirement, as well as background to the establishment of Senior Centers in general. Focusing on this particular Senior Center by the use of its archives, I collected data on membership from the opening of the Center (February 14, 1960) to the present and on member-participation in various activities with a view to understanding the growth of and changes in the Center in its history. In paritcular, I posed the question: Has the Center always been the imitation of a work place as I argue it to be.

2. Synchronic study

(i). Using the archives, I collected data on the membership of the Senior Center at the present time. I was particularly interested in the data on the members' gender, age, previous professions, interests, and reasons for joining the Center. Demographic statistics of the American elderly show that females outnumber males (Belsky 1984). Was this also true of the membership of the Center? If so, had those women worked before? If most of them had not worked except in the home, why did they join the Center (which I hypothesized was a continuation of the work place)? Did these women assume roles characteristic of the work sphere, or did they leave those roles for men? What were the interests of the members?

Were they interested in work related activities, or since they were retired did they prefer home related ones? Did they join the Center to socialize, to perform activities only or to do anything else? Did they expect the Center to provide more activites, encourage fellowship, meet the needs of the elderly, break intergenerational gap, find jobs for them, or anything else?

(ii). I interviewed the elderly and worked as a participant observer of all the activities at the Center in all seasons of the year. I obtained data on various activities offered during each season, and on attendance. Some activities were cancelled in summer. I investigated why they were cancelled. Did this strengthen my hypothesis that the Center was a place of work with its own "summer vacation"? If no activities took place in summer, what did the members do? I collected data on temporary roles people took in each activity as crafters, puppet makers, card (or bingo) players, students, etc.; on whether they added any other role to these roles such as representative, director, president, or secretary during a particular activity; and on how they performed those roles. I collected data on the terminology people used in various activities and in addressing one another. Did they use kinship terminology, work terminology, or anything else? I investigated whether they created "assembly lines" to accelerate what they were doing and whether they "competed" in order to "achieve" something, and whether they expected a "reward" ("salary") in return for what they had done.

Among various activities offered at the Center, there are some "humanities courses" which members can take and learn about a specific subject, (e.g., "land in America," "music and words"). The course is free for the members, and reading material is provided by the Center with no charge for those who take the course.[3] The length of the course is two hours per week for eight or ten weeks. As part of my study at the Center, I voluntarily offered a humanities course entitled "Work and Life." The students had to read various texts on topics related to work such as the meaning of success, self-image, work and ethics, work of later years, etc. Offering the course and analyzing the topics in the context of readings allowed me to pose certain questions which I would have had difficulty posing otherwise.

(iii). The Senior Center offers short trips (one or two days) and long trips (one week inside the United States and two weeks or more outside). I participated in some of these trips, and asked the following questions: Did the trips represent a "Senior Center in motion" or did the members become individual travellers? What motivated the members to travel through the Center? How did they talk about the trip(s) after returning? Did they consider the trip(s) as an achievement, a gift to themselves, or anything else? Did the trip represent work, home, or vacation?

On the whole, the following questions guided the research. How is "work" as a cultural category defined? What does the dichotomy of work/home mean in American culture? What is the "work" of the elderly? What is the symbolic meaning of "organized activities" for the elderly? Are those activities related to home or work? How do the elderly cope with and treat those activities? Do they themselves think they are "playing work," too? How do "work," as a cultural category, and the activities of the elderly relate to broader aspects of the American world view such as notions of time, individual, youth, and aging?

To make sure that the findings at this Senior Center can be applicable to other senior citizens in the United States, I conducted further fieldwork outside the Senior Center. I visited almost all the old-age homogeneous communities in the town where the Senior Center is located, and obtained information regarding their schedules. I conducted some interviews with both the administration and the elderly of these communities. I did several months of voluntary work at the Nutrition Center for the elderly sponsored by the Area Board for Aging. The comparison of this place and the Senior Center provided me with the opportunity to explore the similarities and differences in the behavior of the elderly in different economic and ethnic backgrounds. I also did fieldwork in two retirement communities in two other States to observe the regional differences (if any). The members of the last two communities played the role of control group for my study. While my stay in those communities was relatively short, I duplicated intensively the research of my major fieldwork location. As will be explained in detail later (Chapter V), the results were remarkably similar. Finally, I contacted other Senior Centers in the country such as those in the States of Virginia, New York, Maryland, Idaho, Connecticut, Florida, California, Arizona; and obtained information on their monthly schedules. Comparison of these schedules gave me a broader sense of the types of "organized activities" for the senior citizens as a whole in the United States.

---

[1] The common greeting phrase "how are you doing" has a different connotation for the elderly. Because of their chronic illness, it contains concern for one's health. That is why the response is usually "feel better" rather than "fine."

[2] The terms "senior citizen," "retiree," and "the elderly" are used interchangeably throughout this book to mean a person who is not in the work sphere after the retirement age. Those individuals who have passed the retirement age, but are still members of the work force are, thus, beyond the scope of this study.

[3] These books are written or prepared by specialists on relevant subjects. The books are published by the National Council on the Aging, and distributed nationwide to Senior Centers.

Chapter II

Work, the Central Element of American Culture

The underlying assumption here is the proposition that, in the United States of America, it is only in theory that retirement is synonymous with leisure and rest, and that senior citizens structure their time and activities as though they were working - what I have tried to convey by the concept of "playing work" - is that work has a central place in American culture. The main purpose of this chapter is to show that, first, work has become one central element of the culture, and second, it is through the understanding of work that the American culture as a whole could be carefully comprehended.

A discussion of the meaning of work is, therefore, in order. In doing so, one may obtain a better grasp of the cultural significance of work in American culture if it is compared with other cultural categories such as play, leisure, home, and also with the cultural significance of work in other societies. Moreover, the proposition that, among all cultural categories, work stands out as the most prevalent in American culture, cutting across all subcultural groups and categories, warrants elaborations.

A. Definition of Work

There seems to be no one definition of work. The Random House Dictionary of the English Language offers over one hundred definitions and usages of the term "work," of which the first one is "exertion or effort directed to produce or accomplish something."

Thus, "work" is a generic term. Any kind of activity can be considered work. On the other hand, "work" has special characteristics which distinguish it from other activities. Sebastian De Grazia (1962:246) focuses on the ethical consideration of work. He defines it as:

> An effort or exertion done typically to make a living or keep a house. The activities engaged in while at work all must fall within moral and legal limits, however broadly defined. A man, though a traitor and a spy, may exert himself to earn a living, but does not work except perhaps in his own eyes or those of his hirer (note that *employer* is not the right word here). (Original emphasis).

The criterion for work, here, is not getting a job done or performing an activity, but doing it within the bound of "moral and legal limits."   James O'Toole *et al* (1978:3), on the other hand, define work in terms of its social contributions as "an activity that produces something of value for other people." Nels Anderson (1964:11) gives strictly an economic definition of work as a "continuous employment, in the production of goods and services for remuneration."

Another factor which contributes to the vagueness of the concept of work relates to the technological developments and social changes which affect people's perception of work. In this century alone, tremendous changes in kinds, methods and concepts of work have taken place. New inventions have not only created new jobs and a demand for new types of experts, but also have produced new ways of working. The United States has progressed from a society in which work was primarily task-oriented to one in which work is measured by time spent on the job, from an era of craftsmanship to an era of assembly line production, from a nation of generalists to a nation of specialists. In the past, work was frequently done in family groups, on farms, or in small shops. A son customarily followed his father, whether in plumbing or law they worked together as "Jones and son."

Giant corporations, multinational conglomerates, chain supermarkets and department stores have largely replaced family businesses. This growth in the scale and types of industries has

18

meant a wider range of employment opportunities which, in turn has altered the role of work in people's lives and minds.

One way of describing work is to contrast it with some other distinct, yet related, cultural categories. "Time" can be regarded as a criterion to evaluate activities in terms of being work or non-work. It seems that the time spent at work is usually opposed to free time. De Grazia (1962:64) writes: "...free time means time left off work or not related to work." Thus, free time is not only distinguished from regular employment, but also from the time spent in travel to and from the work place. The question is, now, what kind of activities free time includes. Joffre Dumazedier (1968) writes:

> Free time includes leisure, as well as all other activities that take place outside the context of gainful employment. The personal needs of eating, sleeping, and caring for one's health and appearance, as well as familial, social, civic, and religious obligations, must all be attended to in one's free time.

The passage by Dumazedier is insightful in that work is not simply measured by time restriction but by how the time is spent. The key concept seems to be that of "leisure," a cultural category in its own right. Leisure, as defined by De Grazia, "has always referred to something personal, a state of mind or a quality of feeling" (1962:65). By contrast, work as an activity is associated with anxiety and mental engagement. One has to worry about accountability, responsibility and non-personal "quality of feeling" when one is at work. Leisure, on the other hand, entails different set of values. Dumazedier argues that, leisure includes freedom from obligations and disinterestedness; and it is pleasant and self-oriented. Freedom from obligations means that leisure is the result of free choice. It consists first in freedom from gainful employment in a place of business or study that is part of a school curriculum. It also includes freedom from obligations by other basic forms of social organization such as the family, the community, and the church. Disinterestedness means that leisure is not motivated by gain (e.g., a job); it has no utilitarian purpose (e.g., domestic obligations); it does not aim at any ideological or missionary purpose (e.g., political or spiritual duties). In other words, leisure is not governed by any commercial, utilitarian, or ideological purpose. Leisure has a pleasure seeking nature. The state of satisfaction sought in leisure is an end as opposed to work, for instance, which is generally considered as a means. Leisure is self-oriented. In terms of its effect on the persons concerned, all the manifest functions of leisure answer to individual needs and desires, as distinguished from the primary obligations imposed by society (Dumazedier, 1968).

Some scholars argue that leisure makes sense only in contrast to work. Such an argument seems to define work and leisure too narrowly. Some others associate leisure only with industrialized societies, where, it is argued, there is a clearly and formally defined work sphere. Victor Turner (1978:276-296), for example, writes:

Leisure is the artifact of industrialized, rationalized, bureaucratized, large-scale social systems with arbitrary rather than natural delimitations of work--here it is not a case of the ecological cycle determining cultural and especially productive rhythms.

Considering this dichotomy (work/leisure) which Turner and others take as the unique characteristic of industrial societies, one can conclude that, generally speaking, work is not free from obligations; it is motivated by some commercial, utilitarian or ideological purpose; it is not of pleasure seeking nature; and its manifest functions answer the social needs rather than the individual ones. As a whole, leisure is not a sacrifice, whereas work is.

Another cultural category which is usually contrasted with work is "play." Caillois (1961:9-10) outlines play as an activity which is essentially:

1.**Free**: in which playing is not obligatory; if it were, it would at once lose its attractive and joyous quality as diversion;
2.**Separate**: circumscribed within limits of space and time, defined and fixed in advance;
3.**Uncertain**: the course of which cannot be determined, nor the result attained beforehand, and some latitude for innovations being left to the player's initiative;
4.**Unproductive**: creating neither goods, nor wealth, nor new elements of any kind, and except for the

20

exchange of property among the players, ending in a situation identical to that prevailing at the beginning of the game;

5.**Governed by rules**: under conventions that suspend ordinary laws, and for the moment establish new legislation, which alone counts;

6.**Make-believe**: accompanied by a special awareness of a second reality or of a free unreality, as against real life (Caillois 1961:9-10). (Original emphases).

Some features of play also exist in work. Both work and play are governed by rules, and are circumscribed within limits of space and time. However, its basis in freedom, its non-productivity, and its make-believe nature separate play from work, particularly from the industrial work. Victor Turner (1978:278-96) stresses the notion of freedom.

Sports like football, games like chess, recreations like mountaineering can be hard and governed by rules and routines even more stringent than those of the work situation, but, since they are optional, they are part of an individual's freedom, of one's growing self-mastery, and hence are imbued thoroughly with pleasure than those many types of industrial work in which men are alienated from the fruits and results of their labor.[1]

People may exert a great deal of energy, (even "hard work," or "workout," as they may put it) in such sports as football or mountain climbing, but they do them voluntarily. The same activities become "work" when they are done professionally. The same distinction applies to the sphere of religion. While the ordinary people may participate in religious rituals out of piety, religious officials sometimes do so out of contractual or status obligation, (i.e., as work). Generally speaking, therefore, work differs from leisure in that it entails accountability, responsibility, and public concern; and it differs from play in that it is obligatory and entails producing goods, wealth or services.

Another way of discussing work is in terms of its relation to the work place as compared to home. David Schneider (1968:45-48) points out that work and home are similar in that each is both a place and an activity, but, stresses that they are different in every significant way: "Different things are done at home and at work, towards different ends and in different ways by different people" (ibid.:46). Schneider takes into consideration the "context" in which work is done. Although the work done at home is called "housework" and mothers sometimes complain or talk about the enormous amount of work they have to do in the house, their work is quite different from the organized work done outside home. The difference between work and home, according to Schneider, are categorized on the basis of the following criteria. Work is the domain of the public, whereas home is the domain of the private, and the "boundary is treated with the utmost respect." Work is productive. It has an objective or goal which is clear, explicit, and unitary. What is done at work is for money, not for love. At work, one is hired for what one does and how one does the job. If one fails to do the job properly one is fired and someone else is hired. Thus, relations of work are "of a temporary, transitory sort." At work, standards are set by the technical nature of the job and the performance can be matched against those standards. On the contrary, home has no specific, explicit, unitary objective or goal; "The outcome of home is not a single product, a specific form of entertainment, or a special service" (ibid.:46). Home is not kept for money, but for love. At home, it is who one is that counts, not what one does or how he/she does it. One cannot hire or fire blood relatives. One is born with them. The relationship is permanent. One may not be a good mother to one's child, but one always remains the mother. In case of relatives by law, husband and wife for example, the relationship is ideally permanent. Marriage is "in sickness and in health, for better or for worse, until death do us part." In practice, however, the relationship is susceptible to termination but husband and wife are not employees. One does not hire or fire a spouse. Marriage and divorce are different from hiring or firing an employee. Concerning the job description in a marriage, Schneider writes:

> There is also no technical job description for a husband or a wife in which an output of some product like clean diapers or an earning capacity of so much per week can be set for a spouse of a given age, sex, or standard of quality" (ibid.:47).

Recreation, according to Schneider, "stands midway between home and work and combines the major symbolic features of both" (ibid.:48). Recreation, interchangeably called vacation by Schneider, differs from both work and home in that it is done for one's satisfaction. "Where work is for money and home is for love, recreation is for gratification, to restore, to recreate. One does what one likes to do on vacation." And similarly, a "vacation is productive--of many fish, or animals killed, or pictures painted, or books read--not because these things are productive for money, but because that is what one likes to do" (ibid.:48). In short, what distinguishes work from other activities is that it is a defined set of performances done for a specified remuneration.

Whether compared to leisure, home, or other activities, work has acquired greater significance and performs more functions than simply being a means for economic production. One may even work for the sake of work. It is in this sense that work has been elevated from a means toward a certain objective to an important element of the culture. In their discussion of work, Harris and Cole (1980:261) argue:

> Through the ages, work has had a variety of meanings and has fulfilled numerous functions. Today, work performs five general functions for most individuals: (1) it provides income; (2) it regulates life-activity; (3) it gives a person a sense of identity; (4) it is the source of social relationships; and (5) it offers a set of meaningful life- experiences.

The ambiguity of work, stemming from its broad meaning and usage, and the lack of a specific definition for it, thus, is obvious. Some of those who try to offer some definitions talk, instead, about the similarities or differences between work and other cultural categories such as free time, leisure, play, home, and vacation. With regard to the characteristics existing in the above mentioned cultural categories, what we should note is that no form of activity can be entitled to the epithet *work*, as the term is generally understood in our time (as the collective representation), without being predicated on a number of elements which would be either implicit in the attitudes and social values of those who perform work, or explicitly formalized in its laws and regulations. The most important of these principles are as follows. Work is an instrument to other ends, making a living or generating social identity for example. It has moral and legal limitations. It is obligatory. It produces something of value for other people, not for the performer only. It is in the domain of the public. In production of something of value, it requires standards set by the technical nature of the job. Its duration is of temporary relationships between employers and employees. It centers on money (or something equivalent), not sentiment. One overall observation, however, is that work makes sense only in so far as it is related to "production." In this study when I refer to work, I have in mind all these elements.

B. Work as a Cultural Category

The American social, economic, political, and moral, systems give a broader and more critical status to work than as a means towards an end. In fact, in most cases, the boundary between the means, work, and the end, production of "something of value" has blurred to a point that it is hard to distinguish between the two. A cross-cultural analysis of work will better clarify this point. The concentration on the role of work in societies with different modes of production, namely, hunting-gathering, agricultural, and industrial makes a proper start.

In his article "The original affluent society," Marshall Sahlins (1954:219-240) analyzes the life of hunting-gathering societies as regards the amount of time they spend in working. By comparing some ethnographies of hunter-gatherer groups in terms of the hours men and women put each day in food-connected activities, Sahlins finds four characteristics. First, hunter-gatherers do not work hard. Second, they do not work continuously. Third, they seem to underuse their objective economic possibilities rather than straining to the limits of available labor and disposable resources. Fourth, people pace themselves in such a way that the economy is not physically demanding. Sahlins (Ibid.), thus, concludes:

> Hunters and gatherers work less than we do; and, rather
> than a continuous travail, the food quest is intermittent,
> leisure abundant, and there is a greater amount of sleep

24

in the day time per capita per year than in any condition of society.

To answer the question of why hunter-gatherers do not work hard, Sahlins argues that there are two possible courses to affluence: "Wants may be 'easily satisfied' either by producing much or desiring little" (Ibid.). Hunter-gatherers' way of life may be summarized in the phrase "want not, lack not" which helps them perceive "work" as a means to sustain life and no more. Sahlins concludes that "the amount of work (per capita) increases with the evolution of culture, and the amount of leisure decreases" (Ibid.).

The hunter-gatherers' attitude towards work differs from those in the industrial societies. (More on this later). For hunter-gatherers, work does not regulate their time or life-activity, it does not necessarily give them a sense of identity, and it is not the source of their social relationships. Rather, work, for them has a strict meaning and a narrow definition. In fact, it could as well be a function which hunter-gatherers would rather not perform: If they could help it, probably, they would avoid it. It is easy to conclude, then, that the status and significance of work is a function of culture. A contrast with the status of work in agricultural societies will shed more light on the discussion.

In an effort to determine what adaptations a so-called "primitive" agricultural people would have to make in order to perform industrial work, Salz (1955) made a study of work and life of the Indians in the back mountains of Ecuador. He reports that their type of work and work habits are so unlike the ways and work of industry that almost nothing could be carried over. Salz found little evidence of a philosophy of work or system of ideas about it, yet these Indians work continuously, but in a start-and-stop manner, being rarely impatient or eager regarding work. Ecuadorean Indians work as and when necessary and without "grudging the time." Actually, as Salz (Ibid.) puts it, they give little thought to time, compared to Americans who never forget it. Once more, work seems to be related to the culture, and the cultural mores which value it. The industrial societies, however, see work differently.

So far as work and people's attitude towards it are concerned, in industrial societies, particularly the United States, the picture changes dramatically. One of the most insightful observers to note this was Alexis De Tocqueville (1835). He maintained that regardless of the diverse national and religious ancestry of nineteenth century Americans, they shared a common democratic religion characterized by an intense dedication to productive work and an almost unshakable confidence in its helpful and sanctifying possibilities for both themselves and their posterity. Kluckhohn (1949:233-236), a more modern observer, expresses the same idea in the following fashion:

> Americans are not merely optimistic believers that 'work counts.' Their creed insists that anyone, anywhere in the social structure, can and should 'make the effort.' ...The only way to be safe in American life is to be a success. Failure to 'measure up' is felt as deep personal inadequacy."

In **The Protestant Ethics and the Spirit of Capitalism**, Max Weber (1958) provides us with insight into the beginnings of this attitude and explains the individual's urge in "making the effort" in terms of the notion of "calling," the internal motive that in response to God's call motivates the Protestants to "do" or "perform" something. The rationality of capitalism, Weber argues, is derived from a general rationalization of attitude arising from the reformation. According to the Calvinistic theory of pre-destination, the saved were those who had a genuine inner sense of "calling" in work, with no desire to enjoy the fruits of work. This inner-wordly asceticism oriented the society as a whole towards a religious sense of commitment to work. Therefore, a moral obligation compelled the individuals to perform their function with utmost efficiency. What is worth noting is that according to Weber in the notion of "calling" a valuation of profit or acquisitiveness has very little relevance. "Calling" compels the agent to perform even in non-acquisitive professions (e.g., priesthood) or in social roles (e.g., volunteer works). History has shown that the religious framework gradually decayed and commitment to work became a secular one. Thus from an elegantly worn mantle, work turned into the iron cage of capitalism.

Although very insightful, Weber's anlysis cannot totally be applied to American culture. Preoccupation of Americans with work exceeds far beyond the notion of "calling" in Protestantism. The population of the United States consists of immigrants from all over the world with variety of ethnic, cultural and religious backgrounds. Yet upon their arrival in this land, the immigrants are immersed in what is generally known as "the American way of life," in which work is valued enormously.

A more crystalized account of the importance of work in American culture is found in **Work in America**, by James o'Toole *et al* (1978) who show the importance of work in American culture, and particularly its contribution to people's self-esteem: "Work is a powerful force in shaping a person's sense of identity " (1978:6). The reason, they argue, is that (Ibid.:7):

> The opposite of work [in the United States] is not leisure or free time; it is being victimized by some kind of disorder which, at its extreme, is chaos. It means being unable to plan or predict. And it is precisely in the relation between the desire for order and its achievement that work provides the sense of mastery so important to self-esteem.

Another way of arguing the same point is by considering what happens to those who are outside the work sphere. The absence of work-related identification inflicts traumatic crisis for those who find themselves outside the mainstreem of work force. Note the following two examples. (1) Welfare recipients become "nobodies" as Studs Terkel's interview with a mother of five (forced to go on welfare after being abandoned by her husband), shows (Terkel 1972:303-04). The mother says: "Welfare makes you feel like you are nothing. Like you're laying back and not doing anything and it's falling in your lap. But you must understand, mothers, too, work." (2) The retirees are another example and they suffer a crucial loss of identity (Wilensky, 1966).

The retirees provide a powerful case for the study of the place of work in American Culture. Whereas welfare recipients may, at any given time, enter the work sphere, the retirees, recognized by the society as "the senior citizens," are excluded from the work sphere altogether. The way in which they cope with the loss of identity provides one of the most significant insights in understanding American culture. Being outside the work sphere, their behavior and the way in which they manage their time will show where work as a "powerful force in shaping a person's sense of identity" persists. But before treating this issue, and in order to answer any concern which may raise the issue of the behavior of elderly in other cultures, let's see what kind of activities the elderly have in other societies.

C. A Cross-cultural Analysis of the Activities of the Elderly

Anthropological studies on the elderly show that in some societies, there is no abrupt break from work by means of mandatory retirement. Smith (1961:95-100) reports about the rural Japanese society that upon completion of one's sixtieth year of age, the society provides the individual with the means for "**voluntary** retirement from responsibility" (Ibid., emphasis added). Similarly, as Colleen Rustom (1961:100-103) reports, among the Burmese:

> There is no definite age for retiring for those engaged
> in agriculture where much depends upon the constitution
> and the inclination of the cultivator. His is a gradual
> withdrawal from active life. This is also true of most
> craftsmen who gradually hand over their work to their
> assistants until the time that they 'no longer work.'

As regards the activities in later life, Smith (1961:95-100) mentions the followings for the Japanese elderly: advising their children in family affairs, caring for grandchildren, helping out with household or farm chores, and going frequently to the Buddhist temples. The Japanese elderly, therefore, preserve their status as a valuable segment of the society and are preoccupied with family and religious affairs.

Similar activities exist for the elderly in the villages of India according to William Rowe (1961:104-109) the "intensification of household and family duties" provide a full life for the elderly person, and "the fulfillment of male and female roles often occurs **only** in the later years" (emphasis added). The Person responsible for the behavior of all members of the family unit is an elderly male of the large extended family (usually called **Malik**, meaning "owner" or manager), unless he is physically or otherwise incapacitated. As Rowe reports about the **Malik**:

He is the executive head of the family as an economic unit, which often comprises twenty to thirty individuals. Occupational training of younger males in both the agricultural and artisan castes is the duty of the Malik and older males, who also control expenditures, earnings, and labor deployment.

As the head of the kinship group, the **Malik** represents the group in the complex network of marriage alliances; and hospitality to visiting kin is one of his important duties.

In Indian villages, responsiblities of the female elderly (**Malikin**) are as much as those of the male elderly. Rowe (Ibid.) acknowledges that the **Malikin** is recognizable by the large ring of keys tied to her waist: "These are the symbol of her economic role, for she controls the household stores, directs much of the purchasing, and organizes an elaborate comissary." As the **Malik** directs the training of the young men, **Malikin** instructs the daughters of the house in the womanly activity. Religious duties of the **Malikin** are greater than those of the **Malik**. She performs an array of life-cycle and calendrical rites to ensure maintenance of harmony with the supernatural world, and to validate the social position of the family. She also takes charge in catastrophic situations. As Rowe writes:

> Should the malignant spirits cause illness in the family, interfere with child conception, or should epidemic illness strike the community, it is often the older woman who arranges for shamanistic rites or for other health measures.(Ibid.).

Even if the elderly experience retirement, that does not constitute a decrease in their social status. According to Rustom (1961:100-104), in Burma "Retirement from economic activity does not appear to diminish a person's influence within the family or community." The Burmese elderly are involved in domestic activities through conducting family affairs, training younger generation by virtue of their knowledge and wisdom, and paying long visits to the house of each child, grandchild, or other relatives. Rustom also stresses the elderly's occupation with religious matters:

29

performance of "merit-gaining deeds," regular observance of "duty-day fasts," and "meditation."

The cross-cultural analysis of the activities of the elderly demonstrates that in many societies, older people remain deeply and actively involved in ongoing sets of interpersonal relationships, usually of a kinship nature, in which they frequently occupy pivotal and significant positions. In the United States, however, historical factors have influenced the activities of the American elderly in a differnt direction. Historically, America has been a frontier society. As the children of early colonizers grew up, married, and began to establish their own families, they tended to move away from the parental home and find new grounds for themselves in virgin lands. Friedmann (1961) reveals that the large household of extended kinship was probably never the prevailing mode in America. According to Clark and Anderson (1980:14), "the pattern of European settlement and colonization of North America has mitigated against the retention of close kinship ties between the adult generations in the United States." Thus, "...in the area of family life,..., aged Americans find themselves out of the mainstream" (ibid.:15). As a result, the elderly do not have a clear role to play in the domestic (family) units of the society. By domestic roles, I have in mind such functions as assisting in child births (e.g., acting as midwives), accompanying children on the way to schools, socializing and enculturating the younger generation by babysitting and telling stories, commenting on (or deciding) young people's marriages, and performing sacred rituals. While some elderly persons may perform these functions, generally speaking, these functions are handled mostly by hospitals, parents, teachers, media, nurseries, paid babysitters, and various organizations specialized in performing rituals (e.g., churches). The lack of such functions for the elderly are so much that it led Cumming and Henry to propound their theory of "disengagement" (1961). In their study of a largely white middle class sample from Kansas City, Cumming and Henry assert that there exists a direct relationship between aging and decreased interaction within a social system. This theory has been criticized mainly for its attribution of universality to disengagement (Atchley 1971). Yet, the fact that it may be applicable to the elderly in the United States so far as family affairs are concerned cannot be denied.

The second factor which mitigates against the definition of roles for the elderly, in the United States, is the rapid industrial and economic change and the high value placed on "progress" which stop the elderly from becoming the repositories of knowledge for younger generations. The effect on the elderly, as argued by Clark and Anderson, is that: "The aged are a 'lost generation' in the sense that they are carriers of a dying culture" (1980.:15). Another factor influencing the activities of later life is, as Clark and Anderson argue, "the dominant emphasis in American culture on the value of productivity, with work assuming an almost sacred character" (Ibid.:16). As people reach old age, they find it hard to exemplify this major theme in American culture. The institution of mandatory retirement also excludes many people from the sphere of work after they reach a certain age. Even those who are not susceptible to mandatory retirement may experience certain physical (and cognitive) changes which impair their speed and endurance in the performance of certain occupations at the age of sixty-five, seventy, or older. It is true that there are few aged who are still considered to be "productive" - and therefore highly esteemed in a work-oriented society. But the bulk of the aged are not so fortunate.

If the American elderly are outside the mainstream of family life, are not repositories of knowledge, and are excluded from the most celebrated of all cultural activities (i.e., work), what do they do then? It is difficult to generalize about the way in which the retirees spend their late life. However, the American elderly have the choice of joining various local and national programs in order to occupy their time. Some programs, designed to help older people to pass their time, are those that recruit retirees for a continuation of work, with no salary. Among these are 'Retired Senior Volunteer Program' (RSVP), and 'Serve and Enrich Retirement by Volunteer Experience' program (SERVE). These programs place older volunteers in a variety of settings such as State hospitals, children's homes, and public and private agencies. Other similar programs are the 'Service Corps of Retired Executives' (SCORE) and 'the International Executives Service Corps', both of which attract retired executives to help small businesses; the Teacher Corps, which uses retired teachers to help disadvantaged children; and Operation Green Thumb and Green Light, which employ low-income rural elderly (Manney, 1975:84-85).

Some programs are designed to create a "home" environment for the elderly while working. The "Foster Grandparent" program employs the elderly to work with children in State hospitals and other child-serving institutions. The "Senior Companion" program enables older persons to meet special needs of other older adults, particularly those elderly who reside in their own homes, in nursing homes, or in other institutions.

Another important institution which makes a fascinating subject of anthropological study on American culture is the institution of the senior citizen centers. In the forty years since the senior center "movement" began in New York City, centers have appeared in every sizable city. The typical center offers several recreational and educational programs, besides one or two community services or counselling programs (Ibid.:84-85). Unlike other programs mentioned above, the senior centers are established totally as social, educational, and recreational settings rather than recruiting the elderly to do a specific job.

The situation of the elderly in the United States, therefore, differ from those of other societies in two major respects. One, because of mandatory retirement, and preponderance of nuclear family structure, retirees are removed from the mainstream of active social life. Two, a variety of institutions are set up to provide activities for the elderly. An important question which arises here is how the elderly utilize these institutions and for what purpose. This comprises the main concern of the present work. Before presenting the ethnographic data and their analysis, the way in which the notion of "work" has gone through historical transformations in the United States will be discussed in the following section.

D. Work in American History

A review of the social history of the United States reveals that the relationship between "home" and "work" spheres has experienced some changes. Prior to the nineteenth century, the spheres of home and work were not so distinct. Both home related and work related activities took place in one place called the "household." In other words, home and work in the sense of both the location and the activities themselves were combined. In their discussion of the colonial family in North America, Queen and Habenstein (1961: 294-329) numerate some of the economic functions of the household as follows:

32

Both in New England and in the South,..., the most important economic unit was the household rather than the family. Under the direction of the father and master many sorts of work were carried on - tilling the soil, raising livestock, erecting buildings, and making and repairing vehicles and implements. His wife often supervised spinning, weaving, sewing, cooking, preserving, soap making, and other domestic arts.

The advent of industrialization in the early half of the nineteenth century greatly influenced the development of what is now called "home" and "work" spheres (Johnson 1978; Wallace 1980; Mathaei 1982). The domestic sphere was distinguished from the public sphere. To borrow Marx's distinctions (1977), the spheres of "use" and "exchange" values became distinct. The production for "use" and consumption took place in the home sphere, whereas the production for "exchange" took place in the work sphere.

The distinction still proves to be valid. The "office" or the "work" sphere is considered separate from, yet complementary to, the "home" sphere. As already argued (Chapter I), such a distinction seems to be more clear-cut for younger people and adults in the society than for senior citizens who are assumed to be outside the work sphere.

Historically, in early America people scarcely "retired" in the modern sense of the word. They worked as long as their physical ability permitted. Certain changes and social events in the nineteenth and twentieth centuries led to the need for the official elimination of the elderly from the sphere of work. Some of these changes were as follows: the steady expansion of a new industrial order which preferred younger workers, the rising wave of immigration which reached its height in the first decade of the twentieth century bringing a great many workers to the United States, and the deep economic depressions of the 1890's and 1930's when twenty-five percent of American workers lost their jobs. As Fischer (1977:135) reports:

Forced retirement at a fixed age was very rare in early America, and first appeared for public offices in the late eighteenth century. But not until the late nineteenth century did mandatory retirement become common in most occupations.

At the same time, the new economic order changed the face of family life. "Extended neighborhoods" disappeared.[2] The impact on the elderly was enormous. On the one hand, the removal from the work force had deprived them from their source of income, and on the other hand, the disappearing of extended neighborhoods meant further exclusion of the elderly from the family. As a result, the elderly organized pressure groups to address their needs and problems (Binstock 1972:265-280). The lobbying of the pressure groups as well as the prevailing notion of social welfare at the time led the Federal Government to respond by institutionalizing such programs as social security (Lubove 1968) and medicare (Corning 1969; Skidmore 1970). Gradually, other facilities such as nursing homes (Mendelson 1974), Government subsidized housings, senior citizen centers (Krout 1983:339-352), and retirement homes and villages were also founded.

In summary, regardless of how one defines work, the notion of work has gained far greater significance in American culture today, as compared to other societies as well as American society itself before two centuries ago. For most people, it has become not just a means for "producing something of value," but a crucial source of identity, a mechanism of regulating time, and a foundation of social relationships. As a result, the three age-grades (i.e., children, adults, and old people) each generate identity through work, the children by preparing themselves for work, the adults through actual work and the elderly by playing work (or imitating it)[3]. This may be summarized as: children pre-work, adults work, and old people post-work. In other words, children are potential workers, adults do the actual work, and old people are excluded from work. The following chapters will show the way in which work continues to be the source of identity for the aged even though they are formally outside the work sphere. Moreover, since they cannot do the actual work, both because of their age and their characterization in the society as "retired," they transform their retirement to "playing work."[4]

1 Work has not only been the subject of scholarly research, but also has preoccupied the mind of many other members of American intelligentsia: literary figures, novelists, playwrights, etc. For example, note how comparable Mark Twain's (1835-1910) views on this subject is with those of Victor Turner. In his famous story of **The Adventures of Tom Sawyer** he points out that "...Work consists of whatever a body is obliged to do, and...Play consists of whatever the body is not obliged to do." (1876:23).

2 Extended neighborhood differs from an extended family. Extended families never existed in the United States (Friedmann 1980; Clark and Anderson 1980). Even those who migrated to this land, with a cultural background in which extended family was a norm, gradually lost it. The term extended neighborhood, endured in the United States, refers to the elderly parents and their married children, and probably other relatives, living in separate households in the same neighborhood. Whereas in the extended family, all members live in the same house, act as one unit, and their relationship is intimate, in the extended neighborhood, families are separate units, and their relationships are governed by more formal rules.

3 I am aware that following the official retirement, some senior citizens, who have the means and the know-how, will begin a new career. These individuals constitute only a small percentage of the total number of retirees. In fact, by doing so, they are back as part of the work force and the "adults who do the actual work." This study deals with the way in which the majority of the elderly deal with retirement, outside the work sphere.

4 Some senior citizens, however, do almost nothing because of physical or mental illness. A great number of these people are in hospitals or nursing homes. Although there are some activities for them in nursing homes, this study does not deal with these disabled elderly.

Chapter III

Ethnographic Data and the Senior Center

A. What is a Senior Center?

The first question I asked myself, as I started my research, was "What is a Senior Center?" The following is the definition of a Senior Center as provided by **the Senior Center Standards**(NCOA 1978):

> A Senior Center is a community focal point on aging where older persons as individuals or in groups come together for services and activities which enhance their dignity, support their independence and encourage their involvement in and with the community.
>
> As part of a comprehensive community strategy to meet the needs of older persons, senior center programs take place within and emanate from a facility. These programs consist of a variety of services and activities in such areas as education, creative arts, recreation, advocacy, leadership development, employment, health, nutrition, social work and other supportive services.
>
> The center also serves as a community resource for information on aging, for training professional and lay leadership and for developing new approaches to aging programs.

This description points to two major characteristics of a Senior Center. First, it is an institution, and second it serves a particular segment of the society: the older persons. However, it differs from some other institutions concerned with serving older persons such as nursing homes in that it does not "institutionalize" its members. People do not live in the Center. They can go to the Center as they wish. As long as a person pays his dues, he belongs to the Center. Not going to the Center for certain activities, or for any activity at all, does not deprive a person of his membership.

The Senior Center also differs from such other institutions as nursing homes and nutrition centers[1] in that it is meant to "enhance" life for the elderly rather than sustaining it. The goal of the Senior Center is not keeping the elderly alive or feeding them, rather keeping them lively and and teaching them how to successfully cope with the aging process. Although blood pressure is sometimes taken and a nutritious meal is sold at the Center, these are marginal to its activities.

I should point out that despite the fact that nursing homes, and to some extent nutrition centers, are established primarily on a "health model" rather than "social model," they also offer activities. Actually all organizations serving the elderly try to attract more customers and/or raise funds by emphasizing on the variety of activities they offer.

If the Senior Center does not institutionalize its members, but is established on a "social model," and aims at "enhancing" the life of the elderly, does it resemble "home," "work," or "vacation?" Although some activities are similar to those performed at home, the Senior Center is not a home (using David Schneider's criteria, explained in detail in the preceding chapter). It is not a private domain. In spite of the fact that only members are allowed to utilize the facilities (i.e., activities), everybody can enter the Center. Regarding the membership, except for being a senior citizen, one is not a member of the Center because of **who one is** (i.e., not ascribed). One is, rather, a member because one pays the annual dues and meets the requirements of the Center. The relationship between the Administration and the members is not based on "love" but based on a transaction of "money." It is true that in general a Center is a non-profit organization, but only those who become members (through paying their dues) are able to enjoy the facilities. Note for example the following excerpt from the Senior

If the Senior Center does not institutionalize its members, but is established on a "social model," and aims at "enhancing" the life of the elderly, does it resemble "home," "work," or "vacation?" Although some activities are similar to those performed at home, the Senior Center is not a home (using David Schneider's criteria, explained in detail in the preceding chapter). It is not a private domain. In spite of the fact that only members are allowed to utilize the facilities (i.e., activities), everybody can enter the Center. Regarding the membership, except for being a senior citizen, one is not a member of the Center because of **who one is** (i.e., not ascribed). One is, rather, a member because one pays the annual dues and meets the requirements of the Center. The relationship between the Administration and the members is not based on "love" but based on a transaction of "money." It is true that in general a Center is a non-profit organization, but only those who become members (through paying their dues) are able to enjoy the facilities. Note for example the following excerpt from the Senior Center newsletter (June 1985):

Last Chance to Renew 1985 Membership

This is the month that we delete all those from the mailing list who have not paid their dues. So...if you have not sent your dues in, do so now to ensure that you will continue to remain on our rolls and receive your Newsletter.

The relationship between the Administration and the members is impersonal. A large amount of information about the members exists at the Center. However, if one member chooses not to go to the Center, nobody questions the person (if this is ever learned). The relationship is not permanent. A member can stop paying his dues, or going to the Center, and terminate the relationship forever. When a member dies the death is announced in the monthly newsletter, and the relationship with the person automatically ends, whereas the same event in a home will introduce a great many issues, namely, burial, funeral, and inheritance.

The Senior Center is not totally a "vacation" resort either. As David Schneider argues:

...one can go to a resort or a hotel-and-nightlife place for a vacation. There one finds all the comforts of home but **none of its restrictions**. A room is private, the bed is private, but the meals may be taken in a dining room of some size, at one's own table, certainly with one's family or whoever is sharing the recreation. (1968:48, emphases added).

The Center offers some entertainment and travel activities. The time and the type of programs are selected by the Administration, not by the members. If a person cannot attend the program at a certain time, he misses that program. Programs are not repeated because one person would like to attend them. In case of trips, they are also selected by the Center. The news about them appears in the newsletter several weeks in advance, and the itineraries are at the reception desk, only for those who are taking the trips. Transportation, activities (e.g., sightseeing, viewing a play or attending a concert, etc.), and meals (if any) are on the schedule. The travel expenses (except for personal expenses such as buying souvenirs) constitute a fixed rate for each individual. The extent to which a member has discretion over the program is limited to paying for extra service: the rate in one trip may vary for different individuals depending on extra advantages, a more luxurious room for example. Note that the discretion applies to demands of higher than the standard set by the Center, and not for a cheaper service.

On one level, the entertainment programs or trips look like recreation. One enjoys a program which is intended to be entertaining. Among all the entertaining activities offered by the Center, one has the choice of selecting those which one would like to attend. In the case of the trips, one experiences travelling and visiting the places which may be new to him/her. At a deeper level, however, the entertainments or trips are not recreations. They are **structured** as "packaged vacations" that working persons purchase. Restriction in terms of time, expenses, and/or the type of program prevent these activities from being similar to a recreation. As an example, if a member cannot pay for a trip before the deadline, which is in most cases at eleast one month in advance, he will miss the trip. He cannot travel even if he has enough money after the due date, if he plans to stay in a less expensive motel, have a different

40

type of meal, etc. The "vacation"(?) is planned for the members by someone else, in terms of how to go, where to go, when to go, and what to do. In real vacations, according to Schneider (1968:48), "one does what one likes to do." In these vacations one does what the Center wants one to do.

Taking Schneider's criteria, the Senior Center can best be described as "work." Schneider writes: "Work is productive, its outcome a product of some kind. Whether this is an object like a pair of shoes, a service like legal counsel, or entertainment like a theater does not matter." (Ibid.:46). The Center is, thus, a "work" place whether perceived as a service organization or an entertainment place. It is an institution of the public sphere. Admission to it is governed by a specific procedure whose generality the annual dues strongly symbolize. One is a member when one pays one's dues, and ceases to be so when one does not meet this requirement. The Center sets standards concerning the schedule, expenses, and duties specified for each activity. Members are required to meet those standards. If they do not, they have to terminate their membership of the Center or their participation in a particular activity. The relationship between the Center and the members is impersonal and transitory.

For the administrative staff, also, the Center is their "work" place. They make a living by either serving or entertaining the members. They present the activities of the Center as part of their job. Interestingly, they also present the activities as "work." They use work terminology (e.g., council, committee) for the activities. The Senior Center from the viewpoint of the members and their attitude towards the activities will be discussed in chapter four.

B. Previous Studies on Senior Centers

Most existing studies of the Senior Centers approach them in terms of how often these centers are used and what kind of individuals participate in those activities. The main thrust of those studies centers on the following variables: members and non-members, users and non-users, low usage and high usage. Such specifications as marital status, income, occupation, education, sex, ethnicity, religious background, and living arrangements are used to define the members.

Tuckman (1964:474-479) and Hanssen *et al*. (1978:193-199) report that the above-mentioned variables do not distinguish between members and non-members, users and non-users, low usage and high usage. Other researchers, however, report that some sociodemographic variables differentiate users from non-users. One national survey (Louis Harris and Associates 1975) found that blacks and women and those with less income and education are more likely to attend a Senior Center. Schram and Storey (1961) report that the usage of a Senior Center is greater for males and unemployed. The term "unemployed" in the latter study is ironic since the Senior Centers are established either for retirees or for preparing people for retirement. In a study of the urban elderly in a wide range of programs, Fowler (1970) reports that greater use of services is found among the elderly with more chronic health conditions, more formal education, and higher incomes. Other researchers (Britton 1958:67-69; Hanssen *et al*. 1978:193-199) find that users of Senior Center activities report better levels of health than non-users, thus contradicting Fowler. The above-mentioned studies suffer from a number of drawbacks which limit their contribution to anthropological and gerontological knowledge. They describe and simply document the sociodemographic characteristics of the users. Therefore, the results are likely to be contradictory.

In an effort to transcend a sociodemographic cataloguing of Senior Center user characteristics, Krout (1981:339-352) employs the conceptual model developed by Anderson and his colleagues (1975, 1976). This model identifies three factors that are assumed to account for service utilization among the elderly: "predisposing," "enabling," and "need." "Predisposing" variables are those that affect the tendency of an individual to use services. Age, gender, education, marital status, and living situation are indicators of the predisposing factor. "Enabling" factors facilitate or inhibit the utilization of services if one inclines to use them. Income, car ownership, and frequency of car use are assumed to reflect this factor. The "need" factor indicates the level of problems such as self-assessment of health, number of sick days, and need for transportation. In addition to those three factors, Krout (1983) employs a fourth factor in his study of the Senior Center utilization: "informal network support" which refers to the frequency of and satisfaction with interaction between an older person and informal supports such as children, friends, and neighbors.

In his study of 222 individuals, both users and non-users of a Senior Center, Krout (Ibid.) found that Center users were of a lower status than non-users in terms of income and education, had more contacts with friends, and desired more contacts with their children. Nonparticipants, as Krout mentions, "did not get involved primarily because they were too busy or were not interested. This indicates that they had sufficient levels of interaction or simply did not find the idea of a senior center appealing." In other words, these people had "work" elsewhere.

Although Krout employs various concepts to study the users of the Senior Center, his questions are not different from previous studies. In other words, in the same line of inquiry, he is also concerned with the usage and non-usage of a Senior Center. Interestingly, he himself acknowledges that: "a similar study conducted in a different setting with a different senior center population might produce substantially different results" (ibid.). Therefore, contradictory results are more likely to persist in this kind of analysis.

Some studies have gone beyond categorizing senior centers in terms of their usage and non-usage, and have tried to focus their investigations on the "functions" of Senior Centers. In her study of a Jewish Senior Center in Los Angeles, Myerhoff (1979) found that the Center was used as a means of preserving and strenghtening the Jewish heritage of the members. It seems to me that she would have come to a similar conclusion had she studied any other Center with an exclusive membership of a particular religious or ethnic group.

As already mentioned (chapter I), Hanssen *et al.* (1973:193-199) and Krout (1983:339-352) suggest that Senior Centers function primarily as social and recreational settings. The present research suggests that Senior Centers function primarily because they are imitations of work places. In other words, the more the activities are similar to "work" the more they are welcomed by members. This study, therefore, focuses mostly on the nature of activities offered by the Center and the way in which they are perceived and performed by members. In the next section, I will present the ethnographic data of the Senior Center I studied concerning its historical background, administration and finance, and membership. The sources of information are primarily local newspapers and brochures of the Senior Center itself.

As already mentioned (chapter I), Hanssen *et al.* (1973:193-199) and Krout (1983:339-352) suggest that Senior Centers function primarily as social and recreational settings. The present research suggests that Senior Centers function primarily because they are imitations of work places. In other words, the more the activities are similar to "work" the more they are welcomed by members. This study, therefore, focuses mostly on the nature of activities offered by the Center and the way in which they are perceived and performed by members. In the next section, I will present the ethnographic data of the Senior Center I studied concerning its historical background, administration and finance, and membership. The sources of information are primarily local newspapers and brochures of the Senior Center itself.

C. Historical Background

In the late 1950's a project-funding committee of the "Junior League" was formed to determine the need for a Senior Center in the city concerned and the surrounding areas. Positive fundings led this committee to propose such a project to the membership in November of 1958. Search for a suitable and easy-to-reach location was begun and League representatives attended a hearing of the State Commission on Aging in the capital of the State. Locally, members met with Carol James,[2] of the city's Recreation Department, who helped them plan for such a Center. The League's responsibilities were to include the rental, furnishing, and utilities of a house and the volunteer services of transportation to and from as well as staffing of the Center.

Opening in February 1960, the Senior Center offered a place for those over fifty from 10 a.m. to 4 p.m. on weekdays where they could meet with friends, read, play games, and pursue hobbies. As soon as they settled in, the members also began to offer community services such as stuffing envelopes, packing cancer kits, making Pinkie Puppets for children entering the main local hospital, soliciting for charitable health drives, and making terrariums for the B. R. Sanitarium.

By its third anniversary, the Center found itself with over ninety members and increasing community interest. Because of the latter, while agreeing to continue funding for a fourth year, the League decided to help the Center incorporate as a non-profit self-governing agency. By its fourth year, with its own governing body, the Center was a full member of the United Giver Fund, now the United Way, which covered almost three-fourths of the Center operating expenses, while the remainder was collected from membership dues, donations, and special events. Presently, the Senior Center offers a place and variety of activities to those over fifty-five years of age from 9:30 a.m. to 4:00 p.m. The membership has grown to over 1100. The increasing growth of the membership warranted the establishment of another Center in a nearby town. The new Center, usually referred to as the "satellite," is an adjunct institution which operates under the auspices of the Senior Center. Similar to the latter, it also offers programs but only once a week.

The broader purposes of the Senior Center are explicitly distinguished by Center as "goals" and "objectives." The goals are enumerated as follows:

1- To provide opportunities for the elderly in Planning District 10 (the City and five counties in the State) to fulfill social, cultural, physical and educational needs.

2- To maintain and enhance the personal functioning of elderly people in Planning District 10.

3- To minimize alienation and isolation among the elderly in the community.

And the "objectives" of the Senior Center are known as:

1-To maintain a diverse program of physical, social and cultural activities.
2-To promote socialization among the elderly through various classes, group projects and travel.

3-To educate the elderly about available resources in the community.
4-To involve seniors in the planning and implementation of programs and services for the elderly through the Board and Corps of volunteers."

D. Administration and Finance

The Senior Center is run by a Board of Directors, a Staff, and volunteers. The legally responsible body of the Senior Center, Inc. is the Board of Directors. The Board normally consists of about eighteen members, with six members elected each year for a three year term. All members of the Board are volunteers of whom about two-thirds are members of the Center and one-third from the community at large. The Board is divided into an executive committee and a number of operating committees.

The duties of the Board are to keep the major sponsor of the Center - the United Way - informed on the finances and activities of the Center, to provide a building for programs, and to have proper insurance and bonding on property and people. The Board must keep up-to-date the By-Laws of the Center, and it generally deals with policy and community matters affecting the overall operation of the Center. The specific programs and activities of the Center are the responsibility of the Executive Director who is appointed by and responsible to the Board.

Four staff members work under the Executive Director. The staff include a program director in charge of various activities, a secretary in charge of secretarial jobs, a planner in charge of long-term plans, and a receptionist in charge of answering phones and dealing directly with the people. Aside from the Board of Directors and the staff, there are hundreds of members (and non-members in the community) who volunteer their time to developing and implementing various activities. What volunteers do varies depending on their ability and interest. Some, for instance, do secretarial jobs, some help with the monthly newsletter, some help in the kitchen or in the annual bazaar, and so on.

Financially, the Center is a tax exempt corporation. Its budget for 1984 was $89,393, and its major sponsor, the United Way, supported it with 55% of that ($49,000). For 1985 the budget was about $100,000 and the United Way supported it with about $54,000. The remaining funds required to operate the Center are provided by member dues, the annual bazaar, travel programs, and other miscellaneous self-generating funds, plus special gifts from members and friends of the Center.

In addition to the budget dollars mentioned above, the Center receives other valuable benefits. The Senior Center Headquarters, The Historic M. Library Building, is available to the Center from the City for a nominal rent of $100 per month. To rent similar space at the going commercial rent of $7 or $8 per square foot would be at least $2,000 per month.

Other resources of financial support are matching grants from the Perry Foundation and the General Electric Foundation. These grants, plus the matching funds, raised from membership, plus interest over the past several years now equal to a total of about $200,000.

E. Membership

Census data for the city and the county area reveal a growing population of elderly persons. In 1980, the county was home to 8,548 elderly persons (55+), 15% of its total population. This figure represents a 47% increase over the 1970 elderly population of the county (5,829). While not growing so drastically in total population or in numbers of elderly, the city has experienced a growth in persons aged 55 and over. In 1970 the population of older persons in the city (55+) was 7,056. In 1980 it rose to 7,836 representing an almost 9% increase.

The 1980 census data record a total of 27,116 persons aged 55 and over in all of Planning District 10. The population is distributed in the city and five neighboring counties as follows: the city 7,836 and the counties of A. 8,548, F. 2,197, G. 1,299, L. 4,082, N. 3,154. The A. County urban ring surrounding the City contains 1,839 older persons. Together with the City's elderly, this population comprises 35% of the Planning District's older population.

While the Senior Center considers the entire Planning District its service area, in fact, the vast majority of its membership is concentrated in the City and the urban ring surrounding it. This population of 9,675 persons constitutes 10% of the total population of the City and A. County. Thus, while open to serving the entire planning district, the Senior Center tends to draw its membership primarily from the almost 10,000 older persons in the City and the A. County urban ring.

Concerning the actual number of members, over the last 14 years, membership in the Center has increased from less than 200 to over 1,100. Attendance at Center activities has similarly increased. Records show that during 1979 about 7,500 persons attended Senior Center activities; in 1984 a total of about 18,500 senior citizens participated in the various programs. (These numbers also indicate individuals who attended more than one program). Depending on the nature of the activity, the Center draws anywhere from eight individuals to a language class or craft project to two hundred members at a monthly birthday party.

The membership at the Center is open to everyone over the age of fifty five. The annual membership fee is twelve dollars for individuals and twenty-two dollars for couples (1986). The fee covers most of the activities. Meals provided by the Center and all trips cost separately. Each person should pay for them at the time of use.

To join the Center, every member fills out an application form including his or her name, birth date, doctor's name, the name of a person to be notified in case of emergency, and eight questions about the interests of the applicant, the reasons for joining the Center, and his expectations regarding the activities or the trips at the center. At the time of my fieldwork, the Center had 1,100 members. Since I was allowed to study the archives, I analyzed all of the 1,100 application forms. As already mentioned, the membership has increased drastically since the establishment of the Center. One must note, however, that the population is transitory. As some join the Center, some stop participating in activities for various reasons - moving away, physiological disability, or passing away. Thus, a numerical balance is preserved between those who newly join the Center and those who cease to be members.

Despite this transitoriness, the membership forms a homogeneous group. A comparison between the most recent application forms with those of the late 1960s, does not show any striking difference in terms of gender, age, occupation, or interests of the applicants. Thus, regardless of its rise, the membership has not gone through drastic qualitative changes in the last decade.

Analyzing the application forms was very valuable for the following reasons. First, it contained a great amount of information about the population as a whole. Second, it provided the information about the culturally tabooed question (i.e., the age of the informants) which I had been advised not to ask (see the section on age consciousness, Chapter VI). Finally, the answers were geared towards people's relationship to the Center rather than towards an inquisitive anthropologist. Consequently, their response is less influenced by an outside element, and better represents their inner thoughts.

The sex distribution of the membership corresponds with the general trend in the aging population. Just as the majority of the people among the elderly is female (Belsky 1984), so is the case among the Center membership. Of the 1,100 application forms reviewed, 799 (72.63%) belonged to females and 301 (27.37%) to males. The following table demonstrates the age breakdown of the seniors at the Center.

The age median	Persons	Percent
86 and over	32	3%
75-85	316	29%
65-74	528	48%
under 64	176	16%
no age given	46	4%

The data reveals that the majority (77%) of the membership lies in the 65-85 age range. Sixteen percent of the membership is under age 64. The fact that the Senior Center attracts pre-retirement people is borne out by the data below which reveal that 10% of the membership report that they are still working. While some of the "still working" group may be over the age of 64, it is likely that many would fall into the younger age group. The Center encourages people over 55 (before retirement) to join so that they could cope more easily with retirement (i.e., the abrupt separation from work).

As noted above, 10% of the membership reported that they were still working. One hundred thirty seven (13%) of the female members reported their previous job as housewife, homemaker, or "at home." Six hundred forty responses (58%) of the total sample (1,100) fell into a wide variety of occupations: physician, nurse, teacher, professor, ward clerk, secretary, manager, U.S Government or military personnel, salesperson, self-employed, food service operator, mechanic, laborer, and seamstress. Roughly 35% of the membership worked in what is known as white collar occupations. 23% of the membership were involved in blue collar jobs.

One should note that the definitions of blue and white collar jobs are not precise. The problem still persists even if we substitute the terms white and blue collars to professionals and non-professionals. The division of occupations into blue and white collar primarily serves to give the reader a flavor of the occupational pursuits of the Senior Center membership. These divisions should be treated along the general line that the occupational structure of the members is diverse. The balance of the respondents (19%) either gave no answer to this question (6%) or previously had jobs that I placed into a miscellaneous category (13%) such as movie projectionist, designer, custodian, etc.

The Senior Center application form also asks "Why did you join the Senior Center?" Not surprisingly, one third (33%) of the members joined to participate in the activities. Some of these individuals were interested in a particular activity, still others expressed their motivation in general terms: "to broaden my interests," "to keep busy" (4%), and some sought entertainment (4%). One quarter of the membership (25%) reported that they joined the Center in order to socialize or to be with other older people. Ten percent of the membership joined primarily to participate in the travel programs. Another sizable group (9%) joined because the Center was recommended to them by a friend or relative. A few members (2%, 25 persons) joined to help the Center or be of help to someone. Finally, about 20% of the respondents either gave no answer (18%) or their answers were of a miscellaneous character (2%) such as "Why not?", "Not sure", and "Newcomer to the city ". Thus, whereas the answers to this question are diverse, one third of the members joined the Center primarily for the activities. They used the terms activities, programs, and offerings interchangeably. One can, then, argue that "activities" are the major mechanism that bring people together at the Center.

The image of the Center as an activity-offering place is all the more apparent in the answers given to the following question: "In your own words describe how you would want the Center to best serve our Senior Community?" The majority of respondents (56%) found it difficult to put themselves in the position of advising the Center. They either gave no answers (50%) or requested more time or information in order to answer (6%). Out of the rest (44%) who responded to this question 24% advised the Center "to keep people active" and "provide educational activities" (12%) or expressed their satisfaction as "the Center is doing an excellent job" (12%). Ten percent of the respondents wanted the Center to "Help the needy," "Meet the needs of senior citizens," or "Break intergenerational gaps." The other ten percent of the respondents wanted the Center to "be a place for fellowship" (2.45%), or "offer more trips" (0.72%). Some expressed their willingness to "help" or "attend after retirement" (2.63%), or gave the kind of answer I placed in the miscellaneous category (5.09%): "Get a larger Senior Center building," "Encourage new members," "Make us wear a badge with our name on it," etc.

To sum up, the Senior Center membership is overwhelmingly female, lies in the 65-85 age range, and is structurally diverse in terms of the previous occupations the members had. Concerning why people join the Center and how they expect it to best serve the Senior Community, "activities," more than other things, articulate the point between the indiviuals and the Center ("society"). Not only do people join the Center for "activities," they also would like to strengthen the image of the Center as an activity-offering place by advising it to provide more activities.

The application form does not include any questions on ethnic or religious backgrounds of the applicants. My contacts with the members has shown that although there are a few blacks, foreign-borns, catholics, and jews, the majority of the members are American born white Anglo-Saxon Protestants.

My research concentrated mostly on senior citizens as a group rather than dividing them into male and female for the following reasons. First, the majority of the members (two thirds) are females. Therefore, dividing the group into female and male would lead to an unbalanced sample. Second, of the 799 female members only 137 (17.8%) reported that they were housewives or never worked. The majority of women, 662 persons (82.8%), had been in the work sphere. Thus, the majority of women are continuing what they have always done by occupying themselves with some kind of activity outside the home sphere, in that sense resembling men. Finally, although some gerontologists have argued that after retirement men become more domestic and family (home) oriented like women, I found that sex-associated tasks govern the Center. Women are more interested in sewing and craft projects, whereas men are more interested in horseshoe tournaments. Therefore, I saw no point in analyzing my material on a male/female distinction. In addition to these narrow considerations, the broader logic of my study, already discussed, compelled me to regard the elderly not as an internally differentiated group, but as a group opposed to other groups (age-grades) in society.

F. Meeting Some of the Senior Citizens

Now that we have obtained some quantitative familiarity with the Center and the gender, median age, previous professions, and interests of the members of the Senior Center as a group, let us meet some of these individuals more intimately. Hopefully, that may provide the reader with some insight into the mind and heart of the members. These people are regular and active members of the Center. I have selected these particular individuals mainly because, considering their various life styles, they represent a good segment of the elderly in the United States: one widow; two divorcees; one immigrant; and one couple. These people are not similar in terms of wealth or personal characteristics. But they are deliberately selected to be introduced because they are the type of elderly we often see in our neighborhoods. Disparate information is provided for each individual. The information helps us better understand their personality. The order of this presentation follows no particular criterion.

Miriam

I first met Miriam when her husband, Karl, was alive. Miriam is, as she says, "69 years young." She was married to Karl for forty years until he died in 1985 at the age of eighty-one. Miriam and Karl worked in another State, and moved here after their retirement in order to be near their two daughters. One of their daughters works in the town and the other in a neigboring town. One is married and the other divorced. Prior to his retirement, Karl was a salesman in a shoe store, and Miriam worked in an advertizing agency. She also had her own television talk shows. Miriam and Karl sold their house before moving here. In this town, they rented an apartment. Karl was quiet most of the time. When asked about his quietness, Karl would jokingly say:

"Miriam doesn't give me a chance to talk." Miriam is very energetic and likes to participate in conversations.

When Miriam and Karl moved to this town, they joined the Senior Center and the local chapter of the American Association of Retired Persons (AARP). They were very active at the Senior Center. In a few years, Karl was elected the President of the "men's club."[3] Miriam and Karl participated in the oral history program, bingo, birthday parties, and sporadic social gatherings and parties. Karl had a heart attack while he was playing bingo at the Senior Center. He was taken to hospital, but that did not help: He died at his home a few days later.

After Karl's death, Miriam did not come to the Center for a while. I inquired her about this decision. She answered: "I am busy enough. I used to go to the Center because of Karl. Now that he is gone, I would like to do my own things. I would like to travel, have a television show, go to different branches of the agency I used to work for, and talk to their younger employees." During the first six months following Karl's death, Miriam went to the Center perhaps only two or three times. Meanwhile, she travelled to visit friends and relatives in other towns and States, had a surgery, after which she lost a lot of weight, and had some television shows about senior citizens. By then, she started going to the Senior Center more often. Now she is as active at the Center as she used to be prior to Karl's death. She participates in birthday parties as a guest and as an organizer of some of the programs. In one birthday party she gave a talk and in another she organized a fashion show. Miriam usually takes the role of an organizer. As an oral historian, when she goes to schools, she is the one who introduces everybody. She also acts as a chairperson during the question and answer period. She sometimes helps the staff of the Center by taking various groups to the trips arranged by the Center, during which she works as the leader and the administrator of the group. She takes the people to the motel, restaurant, sightseeing, etc.

Miriam's relationship with one of her daughters has deteriorated since Karl's death. The daughter does not approve of Miriam's having male friends. Miriam made friends with two men approximately six months after Karl's death. One of the men is a member of the Senior Center and the AARP. Meriam shows her affection to him in social gatherings by sitting next to him, touching him, and often joking with him. The other man is a retired businessman in town who, according to Miriam, is very wealthy. Miriam proudly talks about her male friends to the women at the Senior Center, and argues that she likes both, each for his unique personality. Miriam's daughter feels that a woman of her mother's age should not have male friends, or at least not two concomitantly.

Miriam is a member of several age-segregated organizations, yet she is obssessed with staying young: she now introduces herself as 69 years "young." She objects to the people who use the term old in mentioning their age. She finds the secret to happiness in "feeling young and staying active." Based on the comments I have heard, Miriam is thought of as a role model. Everybody admires her, although some women consider her too outspoken and aggressive. One of Miriam's often cited virtues is her busy and active life. "One cannot keep up with her," many people whisper.

Joseph

Joe is in his late sixties. He has worked as an electrician for the army, and is divorced twice. He sadly comments that both of his wives left him because they considered him to be workoholic. The two marriages brought him five children, but Joe regretfully says that he has not been able to establish a good relation with any of his children. Joe blames himself for not exercising strict discipline while his children were growing up. He maintains that he was "too involved" with his job (work).

Joe thinks that the most disastrous incident in his life was his forced retirement because of illness, six years before the official retirement age in the army. He maintains that the decision to retire him so soon was not only unfair but simply wrong. He says that he could have easily continued in his job until his official retirement, because he thought his sickness was never as serious as the army depicted. He frequently repeats the story with bitterness. I personally heard it more than five times within the first year of my fieldwork. Following his "forced" retirement he tried six other jobs but he could not adjust to the new environments. As he puts it, "it took me thirteen years to accept retirement." Being active in the Center and in the local chapter of AARP, he has given up search for new employment. At the Center, he takes classes in Yoga, Spanish, and Humanities, takes part in all birthday parties, lectures, and trips, and finally is one of the active volunteer workers.

Joe is a philosopher in his own right. While with many other senior citizens I had to initiate conversations, with Joe I had no difficulty at all: He would volunteer easily. In response to a simple greeting, Joe would philosophize about life, although he often adds a touch of bitter realism. When asked how he is doing, Joe usually says: "considering my age and habits I am doing fine." Yet he has a positive feeling about himself. He considers himself a person who "makes things happen at the Center." Taking pride in this characteristic of himself, Joe criticizes others for not being very active and positive.

Margueritte

Margueritte, called Peggy, is a ninety-five year old German woman. She and her husband came to the United States in 1946. Peggy's husband died thirty years ago. Peggy has no children, and lives in a room where she keeps it very tidy (I have seen Peggy's place in my several visits there). Of all her relatives in Germany, Peggy is in contact with one niece only. Her niece has visited her several times, the last one being ten years ago.

Peggy still speaks English with a German accent, and pronounces the word "and" as "und." She does not hear well, and uses a hearing aid which sometimes makes a loud bib noise. When told that her hearing aid is making noise, Peggy complains that repairing it is very costly. She likes to talk about Germany, her childhood and youth days. She sometimes takes to the Center some of her pictures taken in Germany. Peggy is very nice and pleasant. Although she has a lot to offer in terms of her personal experience in a changing Europe between the two World Wars, she is not well-received at the Senior Center by other members for the following reasons. It is not easy to understand Peggy because of her distinct German accent. It requires more energy to speak to her because she does not hear well, even with the hearing aid. One gets tired of talking to her because she has a tendency to speak a lot. The members' strategies to overcome these problems are: not to initiate a conversation with her, stop listening to her while she is still talking, or tell her to "be quiet."

Peggy has been a member of the Senior center for eighteen years. Despite her age and hearing difficulties she goes to the Center regularly. She is an active member of the oral history group. Only sickness disrupts her attendance.

Albert

Al is 85 years old. He says that he has outlived his father by two years because his father died at the age of 83. Al is divorced. His ex-wife lives with her second husband in Canada. Al never had any children. When his wife lost their baby before the baby was born because of a miscarriage, she did not want to have children afterwards. Al has one brother who lives with his family in a bigger town seventy miles away. His brother has asked Al to live with them, but he has not accepted the invitation. He says that he is more comfortable by himself because he knows many people in this town, and he can do what he wants in his own house.

Al lives in a house inherited from his parents. The house, a two story building, has seven rooms and several staircases. It also has a garden. Al has been trying to sell the house for three years. The property tax is beyond his meagre income. In addition, Al finds the steps tiring, and cleaning the house and taking care of the garden difficult. Unfortunately, he has not been able to sell the house so far. Every once in a while some people show interest in it, which makes Al very happy. But when they lose interest, Al is sad again. Al has strong religious affiliations, and is an active member of Bible study at the Senior Center. There, he asks others to pray for him so that he may sell his house (which costs sixty thousand dollars).

Al is very active at the senior Center. In addition to the Bible study, he attends some lectures, and is a regular member of bingo, and the Elders' club. Outside the Center, he goes to the First Baptist Church several times a week. He attends the services and sermons at the church. He also goes to the dinner for senior citizens at the church every Wednesday evening. The church provides the main course and asks the guests to bring a side dish. Al usually prepares "deviled eggs" and takes along. Al also sings in the senior citizen choir at the church. He says that he "loves singing."

Although Al knows how to drive and owns a car, he never drives at night because of poor eyesight. He prefers not to drive much during daytime either, because he thinks that younger people do not know how to drive and cause accidents. He usually rides a bus, gets a ride from a friend, or walks to his destination. Al complains that his legs hurt, but as long as he does not sell his house he cannot afford surgery. Al is very bright and pleasant. He is also always well-dressed.

Louise and Robert

Louise and Robert are a married couple. Louise is in her late sixties and Robert is seventy-five years old. Louise and Robert have three sons who are all married and have their own children. Two of their sons live in this State, with two and three and a half hours driving distance each. The other son lives in another State far from here. Louise and Robert do not see their sons very often because, they say, their sons are very busy. Robert is a retired minister. His three sons are ministers, too.

Louise and Robert are very well-to-do, and are considered wealthy by the people at the Senior Center. They own a nice large house. Once a year in the summer time, they invite the members of the Senior Center to spend one of the monthly birthday parties of the Center (in form of a picnic) at their house.

Louise and Robert are so active at the Senior Center that they resemble staff members. In addition to participatig in various activities, they do a lot of volunteer work, especially in annual bazaars and shows to raise money for the Center. In two musical shows "The Holiday Fever" and "Holiday for Linda," Louise sang and played some parts. Robert sold tickets and worked as an usher for both shows. Robert and Louise are active members of Bingo (held at the Center on Fridays from 11:00 to 12:00). In practice, Robert is the president of the bingo activity. He collects the money for prizes, and along with another member, Arthur, buys them. On Fridays, he takes out and reads the numbers for bingo, indentifies the rows to be filled on the game board, checks the winner's numbers, and guides the winner(s) to prizes. On monthly birthday parties, Robert sometimes announces (advertizes) various trips and/or shows held by the Center.

Square dancing is one of the most important hobbies of Robert and Louise. They once told me that they bought their house just because it had a large basement suitable for square dancing. In summer, Robert and Louise entertain the members of their square dancing group at their house once a week. Starting in the fall through spring, they organize beginning, intermediary, and advanced classes for those interested in square dancing in one of the churches in town.

---

1 Nutrition centers for the elderly are also called "meal sites." In some places they are even called "senior centers." These places differ from the senior center I studied in many respects: They offer less activities, are funded by the Federal or State governments, serve inexpensive well-ballanced meals, which constitute the essential reason for their existence, and arrange for inexpensive travels. Usually, their members belong to the less fortunate economic brackets.

2 To protect the privacy of the individuals, throughout this work, pseudo-names have been used for the individuals and the name of places are initialized.

3 The program director of the Senior Center did not think highly of Karl as a president. She argued: "Karl is too old, and does not do much for the men's club." She expected Karl to invite more speakers, and have more interesting programs. It seemed to me that Karl invited good speakers, and arranged interesting slide shows for the club. He even arranged a "spaghetti feast" at the Senior Center, and asked his wife to cook the dinner. More than eighty members of the Center attended the dinner. That evening, Karl raised $250 for the men's club, and donated $150 of that money to the Senior Center.

Chapter IV

"Playing Work," Continuation of Work After Retirement

As discussed in chapter II, in American society children prepare themselves for future career, thus are pre-workers, adults who do the actual work are the workers and the elderly who are formally and actually out of work place are the post-workers. The last group, it will be shown, "play work" or imitate work during their retirement. They make use of many activity centers available for them. The Center under study here functions daily from 9.30 a.m. to 4.00 p.m. Occasionally it holds special events during evenings or weekends. Activities in the Center are numerous and varied. Travel programs included, they add up to 100 to 150 activities a month. A newsletter, mailed to members, informs them of the schedule of activities before the beginning of each month. The members usually brown bag their lunches, but may opt to have salad in summer time or soup and sandwich in winter three times a week, provided by the Center for a small fee. Members can learn or practice foreign languages, make crafts such as quilting or ceramics, play bridge or scrabble, attend exercise classes, listen to lectures, take trips to both local and out of town places and events, participate in a Bible discussion group, and/or aid the community by making Pinkie Puppets, stuffing envelopes and health kits, working with the Red Cross, or visiting the sick and homebound.

Each program appears to be done in an organic form and thus might be referred to as an "activity group." The membership numbers of the activity groups varies depending on the type of activity. The "monthly birthday party," for example, is the most popular activity while the "international affairs" series attracts fewer participants. Interestingly, in large gatherings and during the lunch time (from 12 to 12:30 every day) members seem to form sub-groupings based on their collective experience in other smaller activity groups. For example, the members of the "craft" activity group sit at the same table, the "painting" activity group at another one and so on. This raises the question of whether the Center constitutes a "community." The answer lies in the definition of a community. As defined by Ferdinand Tonnies, community is formed when "the relationship of mutual affirmation...is conceived of...as real and organic life--that is the essential characteristic of the Gemeinschaft (community)." (English translation. 1957:33). The key words are "relationship" and "organic." By the latter, Tonnies means a quality in the relationship where "...change in the position of one will effect the position of the other." (Ibid.:35). Considering Tonnies' first condition, the existence of relationship, the Senior Center is a community. But the interactions among the members do not stand the test of Tonnies' second criterion. They are not organic. In this sense, the Center, as a whole, does not form a community. At most it is possible to argue that each smaller activity group resembles a community, thus making the Center a cluster of various communities. The groups, however, do not form "cliques" in that it is perfectly normal for a member to change his activity and join another activity group or be a member of more than one group at the same time. One's affiliation to an activity group depends on one's attachment to a specific activity and it can easily change. Thus, the most appropriate appellation for the Center, as a whole, may be a "functional collectivity" because each activity group forms a collectivity for a specific purpose.

A. Typology of the Activities

The two main players in this collectivity, the Senior Center Administration and the members, categorize the activities differently. The Administration categorizes them under the following seven rubrics: 1)Lifetime Learning, 2)Cultural/Arts, 3)Health, 4)Social, 5)Trips, 6)Service to the community, and 7)Informational. These categories cover more than sixty different types of activities. Incidentally, the Center also offers a special service to other organizations under the heading of "opened our doors to," which means allowing them to use the building. The activities which those organizations hold in the evenings are not part of the Senior Center. Although the Center takes pride in opening its doors to other organizations, it is unlikely that the members know anything about it.

What is considered by the Center as "Lifetime Learning" includes most of the educational activities such as the "Drivers Course" (learning how to drive as an old person), "Humanities Course" (eight to ten week classes on a particular topic such as "Land in America," "Work and Life") and "Oral History" -- discussing the life style in the past through a search in one's memories). Foreign language conversation circles, ethnic cuisines, and visits to the museums are classified as "Cultural/Arts." Exercise classes, sports, and health related lectures are under the heading "Health." Playing cards, slide shows and movies, and dances are part of the "Social" activities. Visiting various places are under the rubric "Trips." The heading "Service to the Community" includes different services which the members of the Center voluntarily provide for various organizations in town such as the hospital, schools, and the United Way. Discussing such public issues as social security, taxes, and insurance are classified as "Informational."

This list of activities gives an impressive picture of the variety of the activities and the concern of the Center for the elderly. A closer observation indicates that many of the activities easily overlap, and that the distinctions among a number of activities are not accurate. For instance, Bayly Museum tours are considered as "Cultural/Arts" separate from the "Trips," whereas travelling to the Worlds Fair and The Kennedy Center to see products from different parts of the world and listen to or watch an artistic program, repectively, are part of the "Trips." Tax forum and tax advice which both deal with the same issue come under different heading; lifetime learning and informational respectively. Learning how to decorate a cake is classified under "Lifetime Learning" whereas learning how to make a different type of dessert, a fruit basket, is a "Cultural/Arts" activity. Video films and slides are part of "Social" activities, while widows discussion is part of "Lifetime Learning." An important fact to note is that the Center does not consider any of its activities as "Entertainment" even though the motto of the Center is "learning, serving, and having fun." Ironically, the most significant social event, the monthly birthday party, is not mentioned at all. It would seem, then, that the Center sees its activities as a multitude of "services" of various kinds for the elderly.

The categorization of the members themselves differs from this, however. They classify the activities on the basis of their function and utilities. In their view, the activities are either educational or social (by which they mean the activity is an excuse and the reason for getting together). They give more weight to the "social" function of the Center. Closer examinations of their actual behavior shows that this represents what they think the utility of the activities should be rather than what they really are, or how they themselves treat them in practice.

While participating in an activity, members pay careful attention to what they do and, in fact, resent any disruption. Often very little conversation is heard (more on this later). When asked whether they socialize with the members of their activity group outside the Center, the following answer is typical: "No, our socializing is limited to the Center." As to the activities they call "educational," the study of their progress shows that in fact very little education takes place (see chapter VI).

Or take the travel programs, one may think that the elderly travel with the Center because they want to be part of a group. In response to a direct inquiry, they offer other reasons. Most people travel with the Center because, first, they find it cheaper this way. In 1984, a two week trip to China, Japan, and Hong Kong cost only $3,000. Members argue that the same trip would have been much higher had it been arranged outside the Center. The second reason for travelling with the Center is the busy schedule and arrangements which give the elderly plenty to do. The trips usually include a visit to all historic and tourist sites. "One gets to see everything and everywhere," they say. They argue that when one travels by oneself one may not visit many places because of the high cost of the ticket or other reasons, and mainly because one satisfies oneself by saying that "next time I'll go there." The problem with this attitude, as they declare, is that: "There may never be a next time." Other reasons relate to age-associated concerns. One does not have to drive (driving is a burden for many of the elderly). One does not have to find motels, good places to eat, and/or interpreters (in foreign countries). Most importantly, the Center takes care of all bureaucratic requirements such as obtaining visas for trips outside the United States. Socializing which is expressed in the phrase: "One meets interesting people in these trips" almost always comes last. The point is that despite what they say or claim "socializing" figures not very high in priority.

B. Home Sphere/Work Sphere

A better way of understanding the argument, and more relevant to the present work, may be to go beyond both the classification of the Center and that of the members, and classify the activities in relation to home or work. In other words, whether treated as "services," as considered by the Center, or as "Social," as considered by the members, some activites resemble work-related behaviour patterns while others resemble home related ones. The distinction is important in the case of American culture because of the existence of the institution of retirement (i.e., exclusion from the work sphere). What do the American elderly do after retirement? Do they devote themselves to a complacent life in the home sphere? Why are there over 5,000 activity centers for the elderly, in the United States? What is the cultural significance of these centers? Do they offer work- related or home-related activities for the retirees who are withdrawn from the work sphere?

The difference between home and work, one must note, is not universal. As Barnett and Silverman argue the differentiation of home and work "is characteristic of societies in which the capitalist mode of production prevails" (Barnett and Silverman 1979:48). They explain that: "Within the capitalist mode of production, a distinction is created between work (as labor power) as production for exchange-value, and the production of use-value at home" (Ibid.:48). Then they express: "Working in a factory is really 'work.' Is 'housework' really 'work' in the same sense?" (Ibid.).

Marx's description of capitalism starts with his definition of "commodity." He distinguishes two types of commodities: those associated with use-value, and those associated with exchange-value (Marx 1977:126). Marx declares: "the usefulness of a thing makes it a use-value.... Use-values are only realized ... in use or in consumption" (loc. cit.). Marx defines exchange-value as follows:

> Exchange-value appears first of all as the quantitative relation, the proportion, in which use-values of one kind exchange for use-values of another kind. This relation

changes constantly with time and place. Hence exchange-value appears to be something accidental and purely relative, and consequently an intrinsic value, i.e. an exchange-value that is inseparately connected with the commodity, inherent in it, seems a contradiction in terms. (Marx 1976:126).

In relationships based on monetary exchange the use-value is characterized by "commodity-money-commodity'," (i.e., one sells a commodity to buy another commodity in order to use it). Whereas exchange-value is characterized by "money-commodity-money'," (i.e., one buys a commodity in order to sell it more expensively). The exchange-value which results in accumulation of money leads to capitalism. In a capitalist society, Marx views a distinction between "labor" (the person's concrete work activity) and "labor-power" (the person's capacity to work, which is alienated under a capitalist system). Such a distinction leads to the emergence of a domain of contract, (i.e., "work," which is apart from "home," the domain of status)(Barnett and Silverman 1979:48). In the domain of contract, social relationships, between the owners of the means of production and the owners of labor power (workers), are not ideologically perceived in terms of domination and hierarchy (i.e., based on status) but in terms of interaction of "free individuals" (Marx 1976). In a capitalist society the accumulation of capital (in terms of exchange-value: money-commodity-(more)money) dominates the nature of objects (in terms of use-value: commodity-money-(another-commodity). As a result of the interaction of free individuals and the domination of the accumulation of capital over the nature of objects, social relationships are reified as relationships between things: "the definite social relation between men themselves...assumes here, for them, the fantastic form of a relation between things" (ibid.:165).

To divide the activities at the Senior Center, I will employ the term "use-value" for those activities in which the purpose is creating relationships between people, and resemble the activities usually taken place in the the home sphere, the sphere of "love, enduring and diffuse solidarity," using Schneider's terminology. Therefore, such programs as the monthly birthday party, widows' discussion groups, men's club, trips, lunches, and all games regardless of the element of winning and losing (exchange) can be considered home related containing use-value. On the other hand, I will employ the term "exchange-value" for those activities in which the relationship between people is similar to the relation between things, and resemble the activities usually taken place in the work sphere, the sphere of money or something equivalent. Therefore, such programs as the annual bazaar, puppet making for hospitals, and presenting oral histories to schools can be considered work related activities containing exchange-value. To clarify the point, the game of bridge is considered home related whereas the bridge class is work related containing exchange-value. The French conversation is considered home related whereas "beginning French," as a study, is work related. While the Walkers club, the sightseeing of walkers, is considered home related, the travelling of the craft class to a larger city in order to visit and learn new styles of crafting is considered work related. As will be shown, elements of work are introduced into all activities even those categorized as belonging to the home sphere.Two more types of activities belong to the work sphere: 1) various classes taught at the Center (e.g., driving, ceramic classes); 2) inter-organizational meetings, (e.g., legislative forum, Board meetings sponsored by the local chapter of the American Association of Retired Persons (AARP)).

C. Playing Work and the Work Place

There is ambiguity among members as to whether the Senior Center should be seen as "home" or a "work" place. While they view its activities as the best means of socialization, they do not find the Center as a "home." When asked for definition, they describe it as a "service organization which serves the members and is served by them through their work." They, thus, separate the Center from both home and the work place. "Home" for them is personal, private, and full of pleasure. Conversely, work is routine, organized, formal, public, and impersonal. When asked what they mean by impersonal, they say that the work place discourages innovation and hinders one's freedom to innovate. But when told that the Senior Center is also organized, formal, public, and impersonal, members agree but still insist that the Center is a non-profit organization whose stated objective is to serve the community and therefore cannot be taken as a place of work. It appears, then, that the members have three separate spheres in mind: home, service, and work.[1]   The last for them is associated with serious difficulties which they do not face at the Center. Work, they say, is "something that you do not enjoy," "something that you have to do," or "a means to an end." In practice, however, they expect the Senior Center, at least in one general and important respect, to function like a work place: it should provide for them meaningful activities, with something to do.

The most significant reason that the Senior Center is important for the members is precisely that it offers things to do. People do not go there unless they participate in an activity, do volunteer work, ask a question, etc. The Administration does not object to the presence of those members who would like to go to the Center in order to chat and pass time. It even encourages them, in its monthly newsletter, to make use of the Center in hot summer days to enjoy a cool place and to relax, or in cold winter days to enjoy a warm place. Rarely are there people who just "hang around." When asked whether they would ever go to the Center if it did not offer any activity, the members almost always reply "No." The history of the Center also shows that there is a correspondence between membership and the volume of the activities; as the volume of the activities offered by the Center has increased, the membership has grown accordingly.

Compared to others, some activities (e.g., monthly birthday party and the elders' club) usually offer more interesting programs and attract a bigger crowd of people. "Monthly birthday parties" are held once a month from 12:00 to 2:00 p.m. All members are invited and welcomed to attend. Nevertheless, depending on the special program of the day, advertized in the monthly newsletter, the attendance varies from 100 to 300 persons, which is still high compared to the attendance in other activities. Each month the birthday of those members born in that particular month are celebrated through publishing their names in the monthly newsletter, and, in the party, through singing "happy birthday" song to those present and attaching a special tag on their shirts. The party is sequenced as follows: a group of volunteer members welcome the guests and collect the money, a reasonable price, for lunch. After everybody has arrived (around 12:15), the activity starts. The director makes a short speech, lunch is served, and a program arranged for the day (a speech or a slide show) is presented. The director's speech covers announcing the upcoming events, acknowledging the birthday of those who are present, uttering the prayer, and mentioning the sequence of those who will get their buffet style meal (the birthday persons always get their meal first). The birthday parties resemble the luncheons or parties held in bureaucratic companies or government offices. The notion of "birthday" is incorporated into the activity, and its importance is secondary to other organizational purposes, announcing the upcoming events to attract more attendance to other activities, particularly trips, and to present a program. One does not usually see ritual items of an ordinary "birthday party" such as the birthday cake, and candles: The cake is not considered essential and candles (if any) serve decorative purposes on the tables, and are not blown by the birthday persons. The gifts to the birthday persons include the publication of their name in the newsletter, a colorful name tag (given to them to attach on their shirts after they pay for the birthday meal, which also symbolizes that they have 'paid'), hearing the birthday song and their priority to get their meal. The gifts are impersonal in that everybody gets the same gift regardless of his relation with the Center.

The elders' club also meets once a month. Although it is named the "elders' club" for those who have been members of the Center for at least eight years (regardless of their age), all members are invited to attend the meeting. The elders' club meetings are sequenced by having a covered dish lunch (brought by the members), and some kind of a program, usually a slide show or a lecture.

Although both the elderly and the staff of the Center strongly emphasize the "social" aspect of the birthday parties or the meetings of the elders' club, in practice the essential item of the parties or the meetings is the program. Members get disappointed if there is "nothing to do" after having lunch in birthday parties or elders' club meetings. The Center is quite aware of this problem and always arranges some kind of a program. Note the following two examples during which disappointment could be seen clearly. In one of the birthday parties the executive director had taken some members on a trip to Australia and New Zealand. Therefore, other staff were to run the birthday party. The lunch was catered by an Indian restaurant in town and after lunch the restaurant owner was going to display some clothes and decorational items from India, on a table in the corner of the room. I had a feeling that members might not consider the display as some kind of a program. So, I approached one of the staff members and mentioned that the problem might be solved if the Indian lady turned the display into a presentation about Indian culture by showing her items one by one, and describing their usage. The Indian lady refused to do so because, she claimed, she had not prepared a speech. Therefore, the members had an Indian lunch and a look at the display. Later when I asked some of them about the birthday party, they all expressed their disappointment that there was nothing going on. Some even raised the issue with the executive director when she returned from the trip.

The second example relates to the case of changing the location of the party. Birthday parties are held in a local church, not at the Center, because the largest room in the Center can accomodate only seventy persons. As mentioned above, birthday parties are often attended by 100 to 300 persons. Three wealthy members offer monthly birthday parties to be celebrated in their gardens. Such parties resemble an outdoor picnic from 4 to 7 p.m. The sequence, however, is not different from that of a party held indoors, and it includes the director's speech, the meal, and a program. In June 1985, it rained on the appointed day, and the party had to be held in the church. The program (playing bingo) had to be cancelled because the church bans any activity which resembles gambling. Although people understood the church's policy, they were very disappointed. As soons as word about the prohibition of bingo was spread, irritation became apparent. Some blamed themselves for leaving their house (on such a rainy day), others wondered what to do. The crisis was only aborted by a substitute program. Everybody was given two small numbered tickets, one red and one gray. After the meal (i.e., the regular time of the programs), one person walked up to the podium, took the red tickets one by one out of a box, and read the numbers. Those whose number matched the number that was called got a prize (candies, potato chips, cookies, etc.). When the reading of one set of the tickets (the red ones) was over, the process was repeated for the other set of the tickets (the gray ones). In the end everybody got two prizes. It is true that nobody played bingo, but people left happily. They had participated in something. After the first round of reading the numbers, people had realized that each person would get something. But getting something was not as important as the anticipation and excitement for one's number to come out of the box.

Not only do people want an activity or a program to accompany their social gatherings, but they also prefer to be involved and to participate in the activity rather than watching something or listening to someone. Participation means so much more to them than being entertained. For instance, they enjoy watching a singing performance, but enjoy it more when the singer asks them to sing along. First, some may be bashful to sing but if they do they will be very happy for doing so. Playing cards or bingo (the stereotyped activities of the elderly) also helps them to be involved, to do something. When they are playing, everybody concentrates on the game. No one is allowed to disturb this concentration. If somebody speaks in the middle of the game he is told to be quiet. The socializing in the sense of talking is limited to greetings and saying farewell. People need one another as game partners not as conversational companions.

The importance of doing something and being involved is even more visible in the elderly's volunteer work for the Center and/or other organizations. Volunteers are ready to work for almost any organization. I asked people why they did volunteer work. The followings are some of their answers: "The main reason is to stay involved whatever it is," "It gives me something to do, something to look forward to," "It routinizes my time," "It gives me a wonderful outlet. It gets me out of the building (i.e., the house)," "I don't have anything else to do. Life would be dull and boring without volunteer work," "It keeps me interested in life around me," "There is no reason for anyone to say there is nothing to be done. If there is nothing to be done, they are going to die soon." When asked how one can help others to have a successful old age the most common answer was: "encourage them to do volunteer work, even those who have never worked."

The preoccupation of the elderly with "something to do" extends beyond participating in various activities at the Center. They do volunteer work in different organizations. Some keep themselves so busy that they constantly (but proudly) say: "It is a hectic life." They belong to several organizations, and are involved in church activities and various associations. In my interviews with the members, I usually asked them to name some of the activities in which they took part. A lady said that she was a member of a couple of bridge clubs, involved in the church organization, participated in the church bazaar once a year, voluntarily delivered the 'Meals on Wheels' three days a week to the low income elderly, was a member of a historical foundation which met once a week, cleaned one historical house once a month when it was her turn, went to a doll making class once a week, was a member of the 'Questers', the antique study club, which met once a month, and was a member of a dinner club which also met once a month.

The Center does not resemble a work place in terms of payment because the members do not have financial remuneration. However, it offers things for the elderly to do, and in that sense, it does resemble a place of work.

D. Playing Work and the Elements of Work

I shall now consider whether, in performing these activities, the elderly treat them as belonging to the home sphere or to the work sphere. As mentioned before, the ethnographical data demonstrate that not only do the elderly treat the activities identified earlier (such as educational classes) as work related like work, but they treat even those which clearly fall in the home related category the same way. Elements of work are present at all times. Relationships between people resemble the relationships between things with exchange-value dominating them. Moreover, structural and organizational elements of work such as leader-follower relationships (rankings), notions of competency and achievement, fixed time, reward ("salary"), and sacrifice govern even home related activities in the sense of "jobs" to do, and do them properly. As will be clarified later, however, what the elderly do is not real work, rather the imitation of work. In other words, they perceive and organize their behaviour in terms of work model.

First, note the similarity between the formality and professionalism which rules the relationships at the Center with those of any work-place. It clearly appears in what may be termed as an exchange relationship with other organizations in town and nearby cities. The Center plays a mediatory role, by sending its members to various schools, churches, hospitals, etc., to play music, to speak about their experiences or to do some volunteer work. Similarly, it encourages other organizations to send their people to the Center to teach, make a speech or entertain the elderly. The relationship between the members at the Center and those in other organizations is totally based on work, and lasts only for the duration of the work.

70

As an example, the members of the Oral History group, at the Center, go to a school and speak about life in old times to students by sharing their memories with them. When the job is finished the group returns, and there may never be any interaction between the individual members of the Oral History and the individual students. Usually a professional "thank you" note, from the school, follows the group to the Center. No answer is required, and no one bothers to take the opportunity to initiate a relationship with either the school teachers or students. The school may invite the group (as an institution) the following year. It is likely that both members at the Center and students are different people. In the same manner, when a person is invited to entertain or lecture to the members the relationship between members at the Center and that person is terminated after the entertainment or lecture is over. The Center, not members, usually sends a "thank you" note to that person. Therefore, the relationship between the members at the Center and other organizations is based only on the services each group can offer the other.

The relationship between the members and the Administration in the Center also resembles professionalism and work. It projects a remarkable degree of hierarchy.[2] Although the executive director of the Center is not the "boss" in the usual sense, she and her staff are the only decision makers. They schedule various activities. Members have little say on the time, date, and type of programs, and the selection of teachers, lecturers, etc. When a teacher, or entertainer from a different organization is invited, the Administration consults with him/her about the time and date, not with members. Nevertheless, analogous to a general staff meeting at any bureaucratic organization, there is a monthly one hour "full council meeting" in which the representatives of all activity groups attend and report about their respective activity to the Administration. They discuss various issues: attendances, achievements, problems, etc. The Administration listens to these reports and tries to make adjustments where necessary.

Unlike a social (home related) gathering where there is rarely talk of division of roles, (apart from cultural division of roles based on gender, age, etc., which may be ignored or overlapped in some homes) activity groups make a conscious effort to define roles for each member. There is a primary role for the participants as crafters, bingo players, German learners, etc. Some people also have a secondary role as the representative, president (chairperson, or director), secretary, and/or treasurer. Parallel roles in the work sphere (corporate organizations) are very common. Interestingly, no similar roles found in the home sphere such as mother, father, sister, brother, daughter, son, grandparent, uncle, aunt, cousin, etc.; or the roles found in spiritual places as in the church such as minister, deacon, nun, or priest are ever assigned to any member of the activity groups. In each activity, the members who are elected or appointed as president, vice-president, treasurer, or secretary, regulate various functions of the respective activity on the basis of their role. The news about the candidates or appointees is usually published in the newsletter. Note the news in the newsletter of October 1985:

THE MEN'S CLUB

After the September meeting the following slate officers was proposed:

> Marvin B., President
> Bruce R., Vice-President
> Ted A., Vice-President and Secretary
> Charles D., Treasurer

The club will meet again for lunch at the Center, Friday, October 4. Officers will be elected and the year's plan will be discussed.

Similar to the work sphere, there is first a campaign for those roles by the candidates, and then, the election takes place. Recall that I had categorized the men's club as a home related activity containing use-value. The men's club was created at the Center to encourage more social interaction among men. There is no women's club since the population of women is more than twice that for men (see Chapter III), and it is assumed that there is enough interaction among women. The main scheme of the men's club activity was a social gathering, one morning in the month, prepare some coffee and doughnuts, and let men chat about various issues of their interest. However, it did not take long after the men's club turned into a work related activity. Now, officers are elected, programs are suggested, and funds are raised for the club. One morning in the month, men go to the Center, greet one another, have some coffee, listen to both the monthly report (presented by the officers) and a guest speaker, then leave. This is all their chatting and socializing!

In some cases, there may be no formal title for specific functions. However, one person usually assumes the role of leader or organizer. For example, when the Oral History group visits schools, one member acts as the leader ("chairperson"). He/she introduces the elderly or asks them to introduce themselves, and leads the group with regard to their time and topic of discussion, and decides who should address the questions raised by students.

Another variable for measuring the preoccupation of the elderly with work is the predominance of "work" terminologies in the communication among themselves and in their relation with the Administration. Note the usage of the term "work" in the following sentences: "Bridge is a good therapy for old people. It makes you think. It helps your mind work," "In the crafts room, we work together and learn new things," "I enjoy being with people and working with them," "We are now working on a big project for the annual bazaar." A card on the door of the "arts, crafts, and ceramics" room says: "keep learning, new ideas make work interesting." Terms such as committee, club, president, vice-president, representative, ambassador, treasurer, secretary, worker, etc., are heard frequently at the Center. With the help of the Center, a group of members has volunteered to get information about other members who are ill and/or in the hospital. The group functions as visitors or telephone callers to those who are not feeling well. While one expects the group to be called something related to home or friendship, the group has named itself the "**Cheer Committee**."[3] The committee consists of a president, a secretary, and the rest of the group. Similarly, the activity group entitled the "Money Investment Dynamics," consisting of a group of investers, has a president, a vice-president, a treasurer, and a secretary. This group has a "Telephone Committee" which functions as a messenger to announce any important issue before the next meeting (the group meets once a month).

All members consider themselves as "Ambassadors" of the Center to the outside world. On their trips to overseas the same people consider themselves "Ambassadors of good will." Being an ambassador is quite important for them and influnces their behavior and their choice of activities at the Center. They do not participate in an activity unless they are sure they can do it well or at least perform what is expected of them, let us say, as crafters, card players, music players, painters, etc. The most widely heard excuse for one's non-participation in a particular activity, second to not having the time, is: "I cannot do this kind of thing. If I am the ambassador, I have to do my job right." The term "ambassador" is also used by the Administration. There is a group, called "the Rhythm Band" which plays musical instruments for the members during special functions such as the Christmas party. It mostly offers its service to various churches, nursing and retirement homes, and children's rehabilitation centers. The Administration introduces this group as "our ambassadors of good will" before their show.

Another group, the puppet makers, who voluntarily make pink puppets for the children entering the main hospital in town, has a shelf in the craftsroom for itself in which it includes the material and other necessities for making the puppets. The sign on the door of this shelf says: "For puppet workers only." Puppet makers (or rather 'workers' according to the Center) see themselves as workers, too, rather than "philanthropist friends" of the hospital who are having fun while making something useful to make the sick children happy. The usage of the term "only" on the sign signifies that the groups (workers?) participating in other activities held in the same room (e.g., ceramics, crafts) are forbidden to put anything on the shelf. Puppet makers sometimes take some of the puppets home and finish sewing them in order to do their "job" quickly. They mention that they write down the hours that they "work" at home to report it to the Center and the hospital staff.

Similar to the work sphere, the activities are task specific in that each activity is meant to pursue an assigned function (they include a "job description," using Schneider's terminology). Members respect that assignment and try to achieve it in the best possible way. In some cases, they even reach goals above the expectation. For instance, the puppet makers are expected to make 100 "pinkie" puppets every month. The group makes an extra effort to reach that goal even if it means doing some of the work at home (outside the Center). Similarly, the Crafts Group tries to handcraft as much material as it can for the annual bazaar, or some other occasions. The members of the Oral History group meet once a week at the Center, and prepare themselves for visits to schools to talk about their experiences, and thus familiarize students with the life style in the past. In their weekly meetings, members organize their conversation on the basis of various topics (assigned to them by their chairperson) such as transportation, communication, health, fashion, entertainment, etc. They, then, divide these topics into smaller subjects and have each person discuss one subject. For instance, the transportation topic is divided into airplanes, cars, streetcars, trains, ships and boats, bicycles, and so forth. The Oral History activity is not meant to be research oriented. It is meant to be only a search in one's memories, and sharing the memories with those who have had similar experiences (and with school students). But, the dominance of exchange-value changes the purpose of getting together. Some people read books and do research on their respective subject, and try to be well-informed in their speech. Before taking a trip to a school and offering their service, the Oral History members obtain all the possible information about the place such as the school's history, the teacher's name, the students' age, grade, and numbers. With regard to this information they expand and improve the topic of discussion through research and writing outlines. Similarly, the Crafts Group tries to make nice objects, especially for the Center's annual bazaar. This activity group takes the extra effort of travelling to larger towns to visit craft stores and "learn new things" or "get new ideas." This is significant because the group arranges for the transportation and the costs on its own, rather than relying on the Center.

The concern of the elderly with the assignment in each activity and their effort to do the job right result in another element of the work sphere, namely "efficiency" which manifests itself in three different forms: specialization, time consciousness, and assembly line. At the Center, at least four activities are offered every day. The Center tries not to overlap too many activities so that people can have a greater choice. However, the attendance sheets show that each member rarely attends all or even 75% of the activities. People are more selective or try to be more specialists than generalists. They participate in one or two activities, and are committed to their particular activity(ies). For some people, the participation may continue for several years. Some took pride in informing me that they had been a member of the Rhythm Band for 10 years. One was a member of the puppet making group for 13 years. Another was a member of the bridge club for 7 years. The members' insistence on and their pride in the number of years they had participated in a particular activity reminded me of the employees who mention their experience or belonging to an organization by the number of years they have worked for it. In the early days of my fieldwork, I was not aware of the strong sense of commitment on the part of the members of each activity group. Gradually, however, I sensed it. In some cases, the members brought it to my attention, especially when I was unable to participate regularly in a particular activity because of its conflict with other activities which I wanted to observe. Several times, different members objected to me for my sporadic attendance and told me that attending such and such activity was a "commitment." This is worth noting because members distinguish the Senior Center, a "service organization" as they describe it, from a work place mainly because they see no "obligation" in going to the Center. In practice, however, they regard participating in their activity as a commitment, a duty, something close to obligation.

Managing the "time" is extremely important at the Center. Members are very punctual. If an activity is scheduled from 1:00 to 3:00 p.m., they come around 1:00 and leave around 3:00 regardless of whether the nature of the activity is related to home or work. Their punctuality reminds one of punching the clock in the work sphere. In some cases, they are more conscious of the time when a particular activity ends than with the activity itself. When an activity is supposed to end at 12:00, the group is ready to leave at 12:00 even if some people are in the middle of an interesting conversation. They usually say: "Well, it is time to leave. We will talk about it next time." The conversation on that topic usually ends at this stage since people may forget it by next time or something else may come up. The point about time is significant because the members view their attendance as doing some kind of a "job." They are worried whether they are **on time** or not.

The Administration is also concerned with "time." It tries to offer the activities at the "right time." When for some reason (e.g., the teacher's inability to continue the class on a certain date), the Administration has to change the time and/or the day of an activity, the attendance usually decreases. Considering the broader Americans' time consciousness, particularly in the work sphere where, generally speaking, time starts at one end and stops at another, the elderly's handling of the time is noteworthy. Presumably, the retirees have "nothing to do" and, thus, can afford

76

"wasting" time. The fact that they voluntarily attend the Center, subject themselves to a structured time, and observe it rigorously substantiates the broader thesis of this book that "work" constitutes a crucial cultural category in terms of which the American culture can be understood.

The members also form "assembly lines" in order to produce what is to be done faster. Some do volunteer work on monthly birthday parties; they help with setting the tables, serving the food, and cleaning up after the food is served. The assembly line is especially visible in serving the meal which usually consists of a main dish, a side dish, a roll of bread, and dessert. In order to serve the meal someone is in charge of placing the main dish on plates, another in charge of placing the side dish, another in charge of the bread, and yet another person in charge of the dessert. Serving 150 persons in a party may take ten to fifteen minutes by three or four separate assembly lines.

The puppet making group also creates its own assembly line. The group meets once a week for two hours and makes pink puppets (which look like clowns) by using the material furnished by the hospital. The assembly line works as follows. One person cuts the cardboard in the shape of a crescent. Someone else sews the two sides of the crescent paper together to make a hood. A third person sews the ready made faces to the pink fabric and a fourth sews the hood on top of the face and stuffs it with old stockings. Finally a fifth person sews the gathered collar to the puppet's neck.

The crafts group also makes its own assembly line for the annual bazaar. They sometimes make a quilted blanket in addition to other objects. Every person sews some parts of the blanket. For other handicrafts, each person makes some parts of the product or everybody makes something and contributes it to the bazaar. The group neither decides on the price of the products sold at the bazaar, nor makes any money after the sale. A committee at the Center decides on the prices, and the money is collected for the Senior Center. In this case, the Center is the owner of the means of production. It provides the material for crafts through encouraging volunteers to donate fabrics, yarns, beads, etc. It is likely that the crafts members themselves donate some material to the Center, but it will be considered part of the belongings of the Center, not that of any particular individual. The committee also decides on the prices for the finished products. The members of the crafts group play the role of laborers who work there. Creating the assembly line is the group's effort to make the work more efficient and less laborious.

The formation of assembly lines is also visible in some volunteer works. Once in a while, the United Way, or other organizations, asks the Senior Center to help it with stuffing envelopes. The news is announced in the newsletter along with the date and time for stuffing. Many people volunteer to stuff the envelopes. Before starting to work, they make their "assembly line." Some fold, some stuff, and some lick in order to fold the papers, put them in the envelopes and lick the envelopes. Another example relates to the packaging the monthly newsletter for which the Center solicits the help of its members. The newsletter is usually written by the program director, and published by a local company. It consists of a calendar type page presenting all the activities of the month, and deetailed information in other pages. Around the end of each month, the "Newsletter Committee" (consisting of the director of the committee and other volunteers who are all members) gets ready to collate, staple, fold, and label the newsletters, and, then, divide them into the sacks of 50 each. All these tasks are performed by assembly lines: the collaters, staplers, folders, labelers, and dividers. When the sacks are ready, one volunteer drives the program director of the Center to the post office for mailing the newsletters.

Generally speaking, in the home or in the activities related to the home sphere the emphasis is on their craft, quality, uniqueness, and peculiarity. Such phrases as "Home made," "My own kitchen's," "The secret recipe," "Home grown," etc., are usually expressed in proud tones. This is particularly true about such a craft as quilting. One of the reasons a quilted object is costly is that it is the product of the unique work of someone. Conversely, in the activities related to the work sphere, the emphasis is on volume, mass production, and fast performance of the task. One assumes that the elderly would want to produce something they could claim to be uniquely theirs. The puppet making, for example, provides a good opportunity for an elderly to make his/her own specific puppet. But, this is not the case at the Center. Mass production, and meeting the quota is much more important. Again, it is the work and achieving the result in time which counts.

The creation of the assembly line helps accelerate the completion of a task. Hence the projection of achievement and accomplishment. No achievement is forgotten at the Senior Center.

The Administration recognizes the members' achievements in different forms. Even such a natural phenomenon as getting older is regarded as an achievement. The monthly newsletters and the birthday parties are filled with announcing the news about the members' accomplishments: those who surpass ninety years of age, those married for over fifty years, winners in bowling and/or horseshoe tournaments, leaders in the fund raising of the annual bazaar[4] (through selling what the members had made or donated), etc. Once in a while, the craft members' handicrafts are put in "display" at the Center for everybody to appreciate, and to attract new members for the group.

The members themselves occasionally talk about their achievements. Some consider their trips, either through the Center or by themselves (to visit a relative, for example) as achievements. They speak about what they liked best, what they bought, where they went, what they ate, what the best way to change currency (in trips to foreign countries) was, etc. The projection of one's achievements sometimes goes beyond ordinary events at the present time. When members speak about the life in the past they mention the hard times: wars, depression, the absence of technological facilities such as washing machines, vacuum cleaners, automatic cars, etc. Nevertheless, they do not hesitate to remind the listener that although they had hard days, they "struggled and made it." In games, achievements (i.e., winnings) are announced at the end of each game, and people congratulate the winner(s), or show their disappointments if they have lost. "Today it was your day" and/or "It was my day" are common comments heard after each game.

Seeking achievement creates a sense of "competition" either within the Senior Center or in the relation of members with the members of other organizations and other age-grades (for specific examples of the latter see chapter VI, section C). As mentioned before (chapter III), the Center administers the running of a small meeting place for the elderly (called the "satellite" of the Senior Center) in one of the small towns nearby where people meet and get involved in various activities (directed and scheduled by the Senior Center). (Note the similarity between a corporation headquarters with its chains and the Senior Center with its satellite). Since the members in the "satellite" meet only once a week, activities are performed less often than the ones in the Center. For instance, the puppet makers, in the "satellite," meet once a month compared to those at the Center who meet once a week. This is very disturbing for the puppet makers in the Senior Center. They argue that they work harder than the ones in the "satellite" who would like to get the "credit," while the credit should all go to the activity group in the Center. Similarly, in the annual bazaar or in parades, the members try to decorate their booth or car better than other participants in the event. After the event is over, the comments made on the beauty of the booth or car are repeated at the Center, and any prize involved is announced at the birthday party. Competition among activity groups or the members of the same group is prevalent at the Center, particularly in the games (and tournaments). The one who does not win usually appears ashamed, or constantly says: "It is terrible." The winner, on the other hand, feels proud, specially when other members congratulate him/her or comment on his/her luck and/or performance.

Why does the competition exist? Is there any reward ("salary") involved? The rewards are many. The most important one is the purely personal satisfaction which, in different contexts, gives the person a sense of differentness, usefulness, and being productive. Many of my informants would sometimes ask me to visit their activity group in order to see that they as "old people" are "doing something useful, too." On one occasion, there were talks at the Center to cancel the rhythm band activity (due to the lack of sufficient attendance, according to the Administration). Some of the members of that activity expressed their sadness that they will miss each other. One of the members suggested that they could meet once a month in order to see each other and play for "fun." Others disagreed with the suggestion. They said they would "drop out" if they do not visit other places to perform, and come to the Center just for "fun." They argued that there is "no personal satisfaction this way." (Note that their 'personal' satisfaction is dependent on the 'social' recognition of their performances). Thus, while the elderly accentuate "fellowship" as the reason for their gatherings in their words, in their deeds however, fellowship is undermined and performing the task at hand remains the overriding concern.

In games, the most visible reward is when a person is called the winner. In bridge games, there is no material reward, whereas in bingo, many prizes are distributed. Each turn, the winner gets a prize, but in the end of the game everybody is asked to pick one of the remaining prizes. This is advertized in the newsletter as "Come and play bingo on Fridays. Everybody is a winner." The Administration considers winning as "getting prizes." Bingo is played, as everywhere, on the idea of luck. At the end of each turn one person wins and gets a prize. Thus, the element of luck is involved and the luckiest person is the winner. The game is played several times and several people win. In the end, the force of luck, winning and losing are neutralized, and everybody is asked to take something home out of the remaining prizes (candies, cookies, potato chips). On the level of getting prizes, everybody wins and everybody is happy. On the level of winning the game, only a few people win. It is the latter winning (the "real" one) which counts for the members at the Center, and is considered to be the reward.

Once a year, the Senior Center pays a tribute to its member volunteers on a certain birthday party and acknowledges their service. The acknowledgement is done in a very systematic fashion. The news is announced in the newsletter. Each volunteer gets a letter of invitation about two weeks in advance. The volunteers, as guests, do not pay for the meal on the appointed day. Those who usually "work" in the kitchen to serve the meal are asked not to "work" and be guests (note the usage of the term work). The director's speech consists of many many thanks to the volunteers, appreciation of what they do for the Center, and that the Center cannot function properly without their help. The volunteers are also given a carnation or an award representing the appreciation of the Center. Among the volunteers, one is distinguished as "the volunteer of the year" and gets a framed award.

When senior citizens deal with other organizations, they are sometimes sent a "Thank you" note for their service. The note is usually read loudly for everybody with satisfaction, and the picture on the card (if any) is admired. In some cases, the fact that the senior citizens' service is accepted is in itself a reward. Take the example of the Oral History group. The Center contacts various schools in town and offers the services of the Oral History group. The group always hopes to get invited somewhere. Whenever the program director at the Center announces any invitation, the group welcomes it and considers it good news.

The reward of some organizations is more than a "thank you" note. The hospital, for example, invites the puppet makers to a luncheon once a year. It also sends each puppet maker the hospital newsletter and some other magazines. Moreover, each year it gives an award to the person who has worked more than others. This is why each puppet maker records the amount of hours she has worked, either at home or at the Center.

The final element in the work sphere, treated here, is the issue of sacrifice. Going to the Center is a sacrifice for many people. The Senior Center lacks any kind of transportation for its members. The members have to walk, drive, or get a ride with someone else to go to the Center. When the members are supposed to go to a school, to a nursing home, or sightseeing, they first meet at the Center and "carpool" from there. Those who do not own a car or their driving license has been suspended go to the Center by taxi. In the interviews with the elderly, I found the cab fare relatively expensive for a good number of people. Regardless of the financial burden, taxi riders pay the fare in order to go to the Center. There are also some members who live in nearby towns where it takes them thirty or forty-five minutes to drive to get to the Center. During the fieldwork, I witnessed many people who drove a long way on rainy days to get to the Center for a one hour activity, or waited for a cab in the street for a long time on cold days to go home after participating in a one or two hour activity.

E. Conclusion

By projecting various elements of the work sphere and the way in which senior citizens treat the activities offered at the Senior Center, I am not claiming that those elements do not exist in other spheres in American culture. Of course, one can also view sacrifice, achievement, fixed time, reward, etc. in, say, the home sphere. It is the combination of all those elements in a very organized manner which makes the Senior Center an imitation of a work place, and the activities of the senior citizens replication of work. It is the strong element of exchange-value in both home and work related activities which lead to such a conclusion. Take the monthly birthday party, the men's club, or the elders' club. These were all considered to be home related since the purpose in those gatherings is the creation of relationships between people (especially those who are not in the same activity group), and since the emphasis is on social relationships rather than accomplishment of a certain task (e.g., making puppets, learning a foreign language). In practice, however, the relationship between people is very impersonal and similar to the relations between things. In the discussion on whether the Center is a "community" or not, we learned that on one level, it is a community because the members have some degree of interactions. On another level, the Center is not a community because the relationship is not "organic" (see chapter IV, introduction). Larger social gatherings at the Center have not successfully broken into those smaller communities forming organic relation between all the participants. The gatherings resemble those of various units of a work place (factory or a company), rather than gatherings in the home sphere. More importantly, the people mainly participate in a birthday party or the elders' club to listen to a lecture, watch an educational or entertaining program. The gathering is considered unsuccessful or disappointing without the performance of the scheduled program. The concern about time, accomplishment of a certain task, organizational and hierarchical aspects in various activities stops people from forming relationships containing use-value, found in the home sphere. The social element which exists is similar to that which is found in a place of work.

What does the proposition that the Senior Center is an imitation of a work place and the activities of the senior citizens replication of work mean? Does it mean that after retirement the elderly continue working? I do not consider what the elderly do in a Senior Center, and other activity centers similar to it, as simply another type of "work." There is a metaphorical relationship between the Senior Center and the work place, and a metaphorical relationship between the senior citizens and workers (senior citizens:Senior Center::workers:work places). The senior citizens at the Center are not working. They themselves are aware of that. They even get furious when one compares what they are doing to "work."[5] What are they doing, then? I argue that, while at the Center, the elderly imitate what they have been doing in the work place. In other words, they "play work".

The elements of "play" were discussed in detail in chapter II. Play, as Caillois (1961:9-10) argues, is an activity which is essentially free from obligations, circumscribed within limits of space and time (separate), unproductive, governed by rules suspending ordinary laws, and accompanied by make-believe. The ethnographic data of the Senior Center presents the existence of those elements in the members' participation in various activities. The elderly take part in the activities without any obligation. The Senior

Center, as a playground, is separate from the rest of their lives. No goods or wealth are created for the players whose situation in the end of the game is identical to that of the beginning of it. In many instances, ordinary laws are suspended, and for the moment the elderly establish new laws, which alone counts. Regarding the "make-believe" element of plays, the members are aware of a second reality of the activities, as against real life. Even though, one is supposed to get involved in his role as a president, vice-president, etc., and play it the best way he can. Similar to most other games, however, if a member takes the game too seriously, he is very likely to be deserted by other members.

By the usage of the term "play," however, I am not implying that the American elderly are like children (although they are sometimes treated that way), and thus are incapable of producing anything of value to self or society. My concern, here, centers on the metaphorical similarities between the activities offered at the Center and their performance by the senior citizens with those of an organizational work place. We know that the elderly, more than any other age-grades have experienced the culture and had to comply with its social demands and obligations. Thus, they are somehow possessed by it, (i.e., they display far greater cultural biases than the other two age-grades). So far as work is concerned, being raised in a work oriented society (see chapter II, section B), the American elderly are officially forced out of work sphere, therefore it is natural if they introduce elements of work into their activities during retirement.

---

1 As discussed in Chapter II, David Schneider (1980:46) does not make a distinction between "service" and "work" as two separate spheres. He considers the "service" provided in public domain as "work," too.

2 By the usage of the term "hierarchy," I mean the existence of the features of the formality which rules the superordinate/subordinate relationship.

3 Note that since the relationships among members are based on the performance of an activity, there is rarely any forms of relationship among them outside the Center. That may be the reason and the "need" for the formation of a "Cheer Committee" so that it would function as a "friend" or "relative" for those who stop coming to an activity because of illness.

4 The annual bazaar is organized and executed totally by the volunteers. The Crafts group plans for the bazaar a few months in advance. Whereas all the work is done by them the money earned from the bazaar goes to the Center. Their only remuneration is that of acknowledgement and recognition.

5 In the end of the fieldwork, I tried to find out what my natives (the elderly) say about my thesis and the way in which I have interpreted their participations in the activities of the Senior Center. As already mentioned (Chapter I), during the fieldwork I offered a humanities course entitled "Work and Life" to discuss various issues about work, in more depth, with the members of the Senior Center who were taking the course (sitting in on it). Seventeen members were regular students of the class which ran for two hours once a week for ten weeks. In each session, some other members would join the class on a more irregular basis. Each week, I assigned some passages about work written by anthropologists, sociologists, psychologists, and literary writers for the following session. The course covered such topics as the meaning of success, first jobs, changing professions, retirement, work and self-image, etc.

The last session of this class, more than any other event, activity, or incident I had encountered during my fieldwork, portrays the intricacy of my discussion of work and the activities of the elderly. In that session, I talked about the Senior Center and the way in which I thought the elderly utilized it. I told them that the way in which they conducted themselves and their relation to the Center led me to the conclusion that unknowingly, they treated the Center as a "work place" and that their activities appeared as the replication of "work." The elderly's reaction was surprisingly hostile. During the field-wrok, my natives and I had a very pleasant relationship. I was constantly careful not to act or speak in a manner which might be considered offensive to them. My attitude and my feelings towards many of my informants created a pleasant relationship between us. In the last session of the humanities class, it was shocking to see them react so hostile. In loud voices and almost all at the same time objected to my assertion. "Senior Center is not a profit organization." "Nobody forces us to come here." " We do what we like here." "We are served by the Center, and so we return the favor." "We come here for fellowship."

I then elaborated my point, and by so doing practically gained the approval of all. Moreover, they began telling me about those aspects of their life and career which helped me understand them better. In a way, in that class, we all turned into anthropologists learning about our own culture in one way or another.

Chapter V

Beyond the Senior Center

So far the propositions that "work" is a central element of American culture, and that senior citizens "play work" or imitate work has been tested against the activities of the elderly in one Senior Center. Considering the diversity in the cultural backgrounds of various ethnic groups which compose the population of the United States in general, and the fact that a value is placed on the unique contribution of these various groups in particular, is it possible to generalize about "work" as a universal cultural category in this culture? Does the ethnographic data from one Senior Center in the Eastern part of the United States apply to other Senior Centers in the country and to other senior citizens as a whole? Can one talk about the "American" senior citizen?

How could those questions be satisfactorily answered? During the course of the study, I decided to test my hypothesis against other communities of the elderly in the city where I carried most of my fieldwork, and those of other places in the country. For the sake of clarity, the Senior Center will be referred to as the "primary field," and all other organizations and communities of elderly, where I did extra fieldwork will be referred to as the "secondary field." First, I pursued a study of some other old age homogeneous societies in the city of "the primary field." I visited Old Homes (i.e., residential homes for the elderly), nursing homes, and the retirement village. I also did several months of volunteer work in one nutrition center for the elderly. In those places, I interviewed both the elderly and the administrators. Second, I conducted two short field studies in other cities, one in the northern part and one in the southern region of the United States. There I visited activity centers, but also met the elderly in various clubs and recreational areas, and interviewed some of them in their homes. I also visited organizations serving senior citizens in those areas (e.g., nursing homes, adult day care centers). Third, I contacted more than fifty senior centers in the country and asked for their brochures and some of their monthly schedules. About twenty of them, from various regions, responded to my correspondence and furnished me with the requested material.

Thus, the "secondary field" consists of a study of the elderly in activity centers or institutions set up specifically for them, and the elderly who were not affiliated with age-segregated places. The "secondary field" provided me with the opportunity to come into contact with the elderly of different ethnic and economic backgrounds. This was significant because it was possible to study the notion of work not just among the elderly of the middle economic bracket, as was the case in the "primary field," but also as perceived by the elderly of lower and upper economic brackets.

A comparative analysis of the ethnographic data from both the primary and secondary fields showed that my original postulation about the eldery's "playing work" and the centrality of "work" in the United States seems to hold not only in different regions but also among different ethnic and economic groups. In the following pages I will concentrate on the ethnographic data from the "secondary field," and a symbolic analysis of those data. My main focus, however, will be on the data from the nutrition center and the community in the southern region of the country, because they consist of two distinctly ethnic and economic groups.

A. The "Secondary Field"

The nutrition center is established under the Older American Act of 1965. It is funded and supervised by the Federal Government, and the Area Board for Aging respectively. At this place, and similar places where I have visited, most members were black and a few white elderly who previously had blue collar jobs. Most members came to the Center by free transportation provided by the Area Board for Aging.

While it serves a well-balanced inexpensive lunch for the elderly, the nutrition center also offers activities from 10::00 a.m. to 2:00 p.m., three days a week. The difference in the scale notwithstanding, the activities resemble those I have observed in the "primary field." They consist of arts and crafts, educational and health related classes (or lectures), religious discussions, games, and birthday parties. The monthly newsletter informs the members of the type and time of activities. Each day, there are three or four different activities. Serving the meal starts at 12:00 and the tables are cleaned up for afternoon activities at 12:30. Although the program director and volunteers are in charge of setting and cleaning up the tables, some members help with these tasks. When asked why they help, their replies usually comprise such answers as follows: "I enjoy the work," and "It feels good to do something."

Some members do not eat the food provided at the center. They bring their own lunch (a sandwich) but help themselves with coffee or milk provided by the organization. These people argue that they "don't like the meal, and come just for the activities."

My fieldwork at the southern State was different in that I met the elderly outside any age-segregated organizational setting. I knew a retired couple who acted as my contacts with the elderly in the area and introduced me to them. There, I visited and interviewed the elderly in their homes, and recreational places. The community is located in a county with a population of over 14,000 persons, aged 60 and over. The place is well-known for its golf courts. Although many retirees have moved from northern States and have bought houses to retire in this place, the area is not yet a "retirement community," since most senior citizens are natives of the State. The people I interviewed used to be lawyers, executives, physicians or businessmen. In other words, generally speaking, they were in the upper economic bracket in the social scale. They owned large houses, were involved in stock market business, and considered themselves "fortunate" compared to many senior citizens. Even though there were two nutrition centers and one senior center in town, they were not associated with any of them. Instead, they spent their time mostly by playing golf. They were also associated with various local and national organizations such as Questers, American Association of University Women (AAUW), Daughters (or Sons) of the American Revolution (DAR or SAR), Kiwanis, Network, League of Women Voters, etc. They also got themselves involved in voluntary work, church activities, bridge clubs, and taking courses at the local community college.

Added to the ethnographic data from the "primary field," the comparative analysis of the two extreme economic brackets (upper and   lower) and whites and blacks in the two regions (East and

South of the United States) as well as the study of the activities of other senior centers (see below) provided further evidence to assert the following. 1)The American elderly feels obliged to stay busy. 2)What mostly keeps the American elderly busy is a set of organized activities which resemble work. 3)The elderly perform those activities as though they were working. The following pages constitute the elaboration on those three observations based on the ethnographic data from the "secondary field."

B. Symbolic Analysis of the Data

1)**The American senior citizen feels obliged to stay busy.** As long as he is physically able "Doing" is being for him. He takes pride in how active he is. He always numerates his activities proudly. He also reminds the listener that "retirement does not mean vegetation." He suffers if people (i.e., the younger generation) think: "Retirees don't do anything." He argues: "We are as busy as everybody else, if not more." What frightens the American senior citizen is his association with "rocking chair." So, he works hard to remove the image of an elderly person sitting on a rocking chair. The role model for an American elderly is an active person. Note the following poem, which attracted my attention upon my arrival to the home of one of my informants in the southern State.

The Versatile Age
The old rocking chair is empty today,
For Grandmother is no longer in it.
She's off in her car to the office or shop
And buzzes around every minute.
No one shoves Grandma back on the shelf,
She is versatile, forceful, dynamic.
That isn't pie in the oven, my dear,
Her baking today is ceramic.
You won't see her in the warm chimney nook,
Her typewriter clickety-clacks through the night
For Grandma is writing a book.
Grandmother never takes one backward look
To slow down her steady advancing,
She won't tend the babies for you anymore
For Grandma has taken up dancing.

She isn't content with crumbs of thought
With meager and second hand knowledge
Don't bring your mending for Grandma to do,
Grandma has gone back to college!

The poem not only captures the feeling of my informant, it also epitomizes the role model for the American elderly: "versatile, forceful, dynamic." Grandmother is neither associated with the rocking chair, nor with any "home" related object or activity. The poem dissociates "rocking chair," "warm chimney nook," "pie in the oven," "to tend the babies," and "to mend" from grandmothers. It portrays home related objects or activities in sharp contrast with "work" related ones: "car," "office," "shop," "ceramic," "typewriter," "writing books," "dancing," "new thought," and "college."

The American elderly are engaged in variety of activities: wood carving, pottery, basket making, taking various classes, doing volunteer work, writing life history, playing golf or other types of sport, playing cards, travelling, etc. Even "travelling" is considered to be a task for the American elderly. "I have just started travelling," said one of my informants. I asked what he meant by that. He replied: "Well, I didn't use to travel much. Now, I am planning to take two trips a year."

Some elderly take pride in being "more of a joiner" (or "belonger") than others. By this, they mean that they join various organizations or clubs. In the southern State, I interviewed a couple. The wife considered herself a "joiner." She was a member of many organizations: golf club, DAR, AARP, Network, and AAUW. She criticized her husband for being "less of a jonior." The husband justified this by saying that he was "busy enough," and that his activities were not less than those of his wife. He said that he was taking various classes at the community college, was a member of one of the golf clubs in town, and was active in his church.

2) **What mostly keeps the American elderly busy is a set of organized activities which resemble work.** These activities may be offered by age-segregated activity centers or other organizations. In practice, every organization serving senior citizens offers some kind of activity. The organization can be a retirement home, a senior center, an adult day care center, or even a nursing

home. The latter offers the activities for those who can leave their rooms. Offering variety of activities is the source of attraction for many such organizations. The headline in the brochure of one nursing home, in the southern State, says: "Minds, hearts, and hands stay busy at P. Home," and the headline in a residential place for the elderly says: "M. Manor, a busy place." These are just a few examples of the brochures of these organizations. The program director (or activity director) is the first person to be introduced after the director, in those organizations. His/her job, in some cases, is more crucial than that of the director. He/she is the one who knows how to keep the elderly busy.

Those elderly who are not affiliated with age-segregated activity centers also occupy themselves with a set of organized activities. Their golf, bridge games or various meetings are organized. This is significant in that these people do not have to obey the administrative restrictions of any activity center, and can have the leisure of enjoying an unstructured life. However, they tie themselves up with structured time. I interviewed a couple, in the southern State, who named an "international dinner" as part of their schedule. I asked them for further description of it. They said that, on the second Saturday of each month, they get together with some other couples (their friends), and have an international dinner. The dinner is selected beforehand from a non-American cook book, and every family is supposed to contribute to the dinner by preparing some portions of it. The place for the get-together is rotated among participants. Thus, even a friendly get-together is structured.

These organized activities resemble work. They are task-specific and time-specific. The elderly get together at a certain time to do a certain task. The "time" is structured: The beginning and end is very specific. It is arranged and advertized in advance. The task is also structured. The elderly get together to do something specific and nothing else. Knitting, for instance, must be done during the craft hour. It is not considered polite if one knits during the bingo hour even if one is able to concentrate on both tasks

A survey of all activities offered in about twenty senior centers, several retirement homes, day care centers, and nursing homes shows that the activities for the elderly, in various places in the United States (mostly from northern and western States) are similar. Activities include the following: religious assemblies, arts and crafts making, card games, sport, educational classes, sightseeing, entertainment, exercise (or "sittercise"), and some kind of educational program on one's health (called "wellness series," or "growing younger" in various places). Whereas these organizations may differ in the number of the activities they offer, what is common among all is that all activities are time and task specific.

3)**The elderly perform those activities as though they were working.** The elderly structure their time on the basis of their activities. For instance, if they go bowling or play golf on Wednesday mornings, they view it as urgent as going to work. They try not to engage themselves with any other activity which is in conflict with that time. When they perform a group activity, they try to create an organizational arrangement. Whether in playing a card game or doing crafts (or any other activity) the organizational arrangement persists: ranked positions, a specific time, a specific task, an assembly line, the dominance of competition and achievement, and a reward.

Take the friendly international dinner party, mentioned above, for example. The "time" is structured: second Saturday of the month. The "task" is structured: having a non-American dinner. The "place" is structured on a rotating basis. "Leader-follower" relationship dominates. The person who owns a copy of the foreign cook book for the month takes the role of the leader; he/she distributes the copy of the recipe among participants and makes suggestions about what every person should prepare. Similar to an "assembly line" each participant prepares only a particular components of the dinner.[1] "Competition" prevails. Each person tries to prepare his assignment in the best way possible so as to demonstrate that his/hers is tastier or closer to the original recipe. "Achievement" is present. The person who has prepared the most delicious and exotic part of the dinner is recognized as the achiever. His/her "reward" is the others' recognition and admiration.

At the nutrition center also people introduced the elements of work. Members used "work" vocabularies (e.g., committee, council), were conscious of the time in each activity, assumed bureaucratic positions (e.g., president, secretary), observed competition and achievement, and searched for reward. Bureaucratic positions were especially visible in the full council meeting (similar to the one I had observed in the "primary field," see chapter IV). Competition and acheivement were found in arts and crafts, games, and in the bimonthly program of "showing one's talent." The latter included the participation of those members who had either made or could do something interesting. At the appointed time, the program director of the nutrition center thanks the participants for accepting to show their "talent" (making some handcrafted items or entertaining by singing, playing music, or uttering a prayer), and introduces them to the audience (i.e., other members). The "reward" is prevalent in the admiration of the audience and their applause, and in other cases such as bingo in the prizes the winners get.

In the survey of brochures and monthly schedules of various activity centers in the country, one can also see elements of "work." Work (corporate) vocbularies are dominant (e.g., needlework, legal council, quilters' meeting, newsletter committee). Time and types of activities are organized. The brochures also mention the appointment or election of officers to different committees and group activities. They announce the winners in occasional contests (e.g., door decoration for Christmas, hat making). They also acknowledge the "outstanding accomplishments" of individuals in certain tasks.

The introduction of elements of work is also visible among those who consider their retirement "play" only and have the leisure of enjoying an affluent retirement (i.e., the retirees studied in a southern State). I have already mentioned about the "international dinner" of some of these people. As mentioned before, "golf" is the activity which occupies almost everybody's time. In fact, people are obsessed with golf. It regulates their time, gives meaning to their speeches, and even helps them make judgements about people's abilities.

There are several golf clubs in the area where I did fieldwork. The golf clubs charge an annual membership fee. Some of them also charge for each session the game is played. In addition to providing the land and equipment for playing golf, some clubs offer dinner and dance parties to their members. All the people I interviewed were members of at least one golf club. Some had their own equipments, while some rented them. People could either play by themselves (which they called "practice") or in a group of two or more persons. Group games were scheduled whereas individual games were not as restrict in terms of time. I attended both individual games ("practices") and the group ones. One of the groups I observed consisted of two women who were members of a larger group of women players. The larger group operated under one president and one secretary who supervised the games of smaller groups. The large group (composed of sixteen persons) met once a month on a Thursday morning and discussed various issues related to the games. It also arranged games (including prizes) among individuals or groups.

Before each game, the group signed up the attendance sheet in the golf club and got the relevant papers to write down the scores. The signing up reminded me of "punching the clock" in the work sphere. The paper for scores would report the achievements of each player. During the game both players constantly emphasized that the game is just for "fun," even though they took the game very seriously with regard to the scores. One of the women asked me to check on the other person's shots. When I looked at her with a puzzled face, she whispered that, "she has a tendency to cheat." When the game was over, the players signed up the sheets along with the time within which they had finished the game. There they joined other players. Everybody talked about the way she had played that day. The person with good score would act proudly, but would keep quiet, whereas the person with bad score would constantly come up with excuses (e.g., not feeling well that particular day) for doing poorly. To an outside observer, these people's "playing" golf seems as serious as "work," although they are not professionals in the sense that playing golf is not their job. They try to improve their skill as much as they can. If an unexpected problem, a surgery for example, stops them from "practice" it bothers them greatly because it will take them a while to go back to their "score." Just as they "play work," they work hard at their play. The ethnographic data from the "primary" and "secondary" fields show that even though the American retirees, as a whole, can have the leisure of enjoying an unstructured life, they structure their life by regulated time and tasks. To that end, they occupy themselves with a set of organized activities, in the form of those offered by age-segregated activity centers or other national and local organizations. These activities look "real" to the American elderly only if they resemble "work." They should be dominated by a scheduled time, a specific task, and structural arrangements. Generally speaking, this applies regardless of the differences between economic and ethnic backgrounds.

1 One could make a similar argument about "pot-luck," or "covered dish" parties. The meal is composed of the various "parts" prepared by each "assembly worker" (each guest).

Chapter VI

Symbolic Analysis, A Holistic Perspective

What is the significance of the ethnographic data presented in the previous chapters? How do they relate to the general scheme of American culture? While addressing these questions, the goal in the present chapter is to put the case of the elderly into a larger cultural perspective. As mentioned before, three distinct social groups--pre-workers, workers, and post-workers--dominate American society. In the first section of this chapter, the similarities between the two groups outside the work sphere--pre-workers and post-workers--will be analyzed. Children are outside the work sphere because of their age, but they "play work." They produce "preparedness" for future work. Similarly, the elderly are excluded from the work sphere because of their age. Ironically, they also "play work." What they produce will be explored in the second section. It will be shown that they struggle to preserve their identity as productive members of the society which they were in their work phase. Thus, a general picture of American culture portrays a society in which all three age grades are engaged in activities related to work. One interesting issue remains, which is that of the "age" of the elderly. The third section will treat this issue and also the the notion of "age" in great depth.

A. Two social extremities: pre-workers and post-workers

To begin with, the structural similarities between pre-workers and post-workers show how the activities of the elderly constitute playing work. I have already argued that, in the United States, the three age-grades and their activities can be divided as follows: children pre-work; adults work; and senior citizens post-work. The middle generation (i.e., adults) not only has the burden of productivity but also serves the other two. It is a mediator between those who are preparing to work (i.e., children) and those whose work age is passed and are retired (i.e., senior citizens). The two extreme age-grades, children and the elderly, are outside the work sphere and, as will be shown, they resemble each other greatly. This phenomenon can be seen as a specifically modern Western expression of Radcliffe-Brown's principle of the merging of alternate generations.

The similarity between senior citizens and children takes many forms. The ethnographic data of an old age homogeneous society shows that the Senior Center and schools resemble in many respects: in terms of "time" in seasonal schedules and daily hours, teacher-student relationship, and imitation of "work." The activities at the Senior Center are offered on the basis of a seasonal schedule. Fall and spring are the busiest time of the year in the Center in terms of the number of offered activities and the number of member attendances. This schedule resembles that of school semesters which begin in the fall and, following a break in Christmas, will resume again in spring until May. Similarly at the Center, fall represents the beginning of new activities, followed by a Christmas break. In the middle of January, activities start again. Around the end of May until the beginning of September the activities are relaxed. In summer, many activities are totally cancelled (e.g., oral history, all language classes). Birthday parties take a more casual form. They are held outdoors rather than inside a church building, their usual location. Although the meal is still provided by the Center, birthday parties are called "picnics." In contrast to the elderly and children the working people do not follow this rythmic cycle because they have to work regularly. It is true that most people in the work sphere take a vacation in summer or winter, but theirs is not institutionalized.

Activities are mostly offered on weekdays during daytime from 9:30 a.m. to 4:00 p.m. Compared to the regular 9 to 5 "work" hours, the hours of activities at the Center are fewer. Similarly, the children's school hours are less than regular 9 to 5 "work" hours. Most of the activities at the Center last for only one hour (e.g., oral history, lectures held by the arthritis club, heart saver course, all language classes). Except for trips which may last several days, the rest of the activities last two to three hours (e.g., ceramics, puppet making, humanities courses, afternoon bridge, monthly birthday parties). While the administrators work from 9:30 to 4:30, none of the activities last seven full hours. In the case of lectures and some educational programs, the preference is that they last one or two hours with a break in between so that they will be less tiring for the audience. Day time is preferred to evenings because most members have difficulty or do not like to go out after dark. Some do not drive at all, some cannot drive well at night owing to their poor eyesight, and some simply find it dangerous to go out at night because of crime.[1]

The activities at the Center are subject to cancellation in case of heavy rain or snow. According to the regulations of the Center, when schools cancel their classes due to the weather, the Center cancels its activities, too. The cancellation of the programs is announced on the radio along with the closing of schools. The busiest time of the year, at the Center, are spring and fall. The elderly are very much dependent on the weather. They do not come out of their homes when it is too cold or too hot, or when the roads are slippery. They are afraid of falling and breaking their bones.

The similarities between pre-workers and post-workers are also striking in terms of teacher-student relationships. Teacher-student relationships prevail during the many classes (e.g., painting, humanities, ceramics, bridge, exercise) which are regularly held at the Senior Center. The information about the course (time, fee (if any), instructor) is announced in the monthly newsletter. Those who would like to attend the class are supposed to "sign up" (register?) first, pay the fee, and sign their name in the attendance sheet each time they attend the class. Although not as strict, the latter reminds one of a "roll call." A person, usually a non-member of the Center, conducts the class, assigns requirements, entertains questions, and invites the students' comments. For the person who conducts the class, the elderly use the term "teacher" or "professor" rather than leader, instructor, facilitator, etc. Occasionally, a member of the Center who has a special expertise may conduct a class. For instance, in "French conversation," a foreign-born member leads the conversation, corrects grammatical mistakes of others, and helps them with vocabularies. Similarly, in "Bible study," each month a person is chosen as the teacher to lead the class. Both the "French conversation" and the "Bible study" are referred to as conversation and discussion sessions. Nevertheless, even there, the teacher-student relationship automatically governs. Other special one time educational programs such as those on health, nutrition, art, international or legal affairs, also turn into a class setting. The person in charge of the program assumes the role of a teacher.

Senior citizens act like students, perhaps because they see themselves as students or because they value education. In their membership application forms, some had written "to broaden interests" as their motive in joining the Center. As an answer to the question "In your own words describe how you want the Center to best serve our senior community" the followings were very frequent: "have mentally and physically educational activities," "keep our minds active," "help us learn our individual self-awareness," "help us learn new skills," "provide opportunity for further growth and development." Other answers included requests for various classes (e.g., economics, sociology, ethics, music appreciation).

Some of the elderly take courses at the university or the community college in town apart from attending the classes offered at the Senior Center. When asked why they take these classes, the most common answers are "learning is good," "it makes us smarter." Some, however, take classes because they think they are gaining something without having to pay anything for it: "There is no tuition for senior citizens. Why not?" The fact that these courses require no exams and involve no credits are the motivations for some people. When asked whether it is derogatory or prestigious to compare a senior citizen with students, everybody found it prestigious to do so. To the question of "what do you want to do with the knowledge you get in these courses," most people answered "nothing." It seems that it is the involvement rather than the result which is important for the elderly in taking those courses. It does not matter if they never take advantage of the knowledge, but they always proudly mention that they have "taken" such and such course. Although they do not get any credit in taking those courses they use the term "take" rather than "audit" or "sit in" for attending a class. One of my informants always proudly counted all thirteen courses he had taken at the community college. The courses were not related towards any specific subject or major. They included skiing, bicycle repair, history, sociology, flying, etc.

The image of the Center as a learning institution is also embedded in the minds of the administrators. Note the speech of the

100

executive director of the Center in which the motto of the Center is repeated: "We learn, we serve, we have fun." She continued:[2]

> We have continuous lifetime learning programs--one covers current events beginning with U.S. Foreign policy, one teaches about stress management, another about foreign language.
> We have classes in wellness, teaching how to care for bodies--to eat properly--exercise. We have a mini Humanities Course that explores words and music of famous showtunes.[3] We are teaching members to be interviewers of our Oral History Project. We learn unusual arts and crafts. An example is the beautiful authentic Hawaiian Quilt made by our members.[4] Aside from the money it raised for the Center it was a cooperative effort, a thing of beauty, a shared pride. We hung it in the great room where members brought friends to admire its design and workmanship.[5]

Whereas the idea of learning is strong in the minds of both members and the Administration, learning itself does not seriously or effectively take place. In the case of occasional educational programs, learning is short-term and sporadic. Moreover, the motto of the Center indicates explicitly that "fun" is a very important element at the Center. This is reflected in the speech of the executive director:

> We have fun!!!! Monthly birthday parties--no birthday is forgotten. Bridge games, Bingo, Rhythm Band, Swimming,[6] Walking. Our latest adventure is a Musical Revue, "Holiday Fever"[7] where professionals and Senior Center members join talents to give this community the best musical ever!

Educational classes resemble what children do when they play "teacher/student." The elderly assume the role of students (or teachers) and play these roles. They imitate what students do. They register for the course, pay the registration fee (if any), sign up the attendance sheet, and do the homework (if any). What is intriguing in these classes is that they are based on a "work" model more than education taken place in schools or play ("fun"). To demonstrate the point let us examine two of the activities, ceramics and rhythm band.

The teacher of the ceramic classes is a woman who has a ceramic store in town. She goes to the Center once a week for two hours for the purpose of teaching the art of ceramics. Each participant (student) in the activity must pay a small fee to attend the class. Depending on the number of students, the teacher takes to the Center several different types of fired unpolished objects with tools to finish them. These objects are referred to as "the green ware," which means unfinished product. Some objects have ritualistic significance. They look like Santa Claus, Christmas bells, bunny rabbits, etc. Other objects are various kinds of flower vases, candle holders, decorating plates, book holders, mugs, etc. Students in the class choose the object they would like to work on, and put their initials on the back of the object where it is not easily seen. Following the selection of the object, the "work" or "teaching," as students say, starts.

The first step is the "cleaning" of an already fired product. The teacher teaches the students to remove the unwanted clay from the edges of the object by using a knife, polish the surface by using the "grit pad," wash it with the "synthetic sponge," (a wet sponge) and finally brush it with the "duster brush." After having been cleaned, the object has to be fired before being dyed. The process of "cleaning" takes almost two hours for a beginner. If somebody finishes his/her "work" on the product sooner than two hours, he/she can start "working" on another one. The teacher takes all cleaned objects to her store, fires them, and brings them back to the Center the following week.

The second stage is the "underglazing" of the product, which is not called "green ware" any longer but "bisque." The following week, each student takes his product and gets a new lesson on dyeing (underglazing) the product. Inquiring about the students' choice of color, the teacher gives them the right amount of color and the brush(es) to coat the product. The students' questions at this stage are mainly about mixing various colors to get the desired mixture. Depending on the size of the product and variety of colors, underglazing takes almost one to eight hours. When it takes more than two hours for a product to be dyed (underglazed), the student must dye it during several sequent weeks since he/she cannot take the product and tools home to work on. After a product is underglazed,

102

the teacher takes the product to her store, fires it, and brings it back to the Center the following week.

The third stage is the "glazing" of the product to make it "ultra clear." This stage is required only if the student wants his product to be glazed. Otherwise, the product is ready to be used after being underglazed and fired. The following week, the students pick their own products and wait for a new lesson. The teacher gives each student the glazed brush to coat the product twice smoothly to make it "ultra clear." After a product is glazed, the teacher takes it to her store, fires it, and brings it back to the Center the following week.

The fourth stage is the transferring of a picture or design from a prepared paper to the product ("decal"). This process is also taught by the teacher who provides the picture or design and the required material for students to work on. After this process is finished, the teacher takes the product to her store, fires it, and brings it back to the Center the following week. Altogether, there are four stages for an already made product to be finished: cleaning, underglazing, glazing, and decal. The product has to be fired in between each stage. The last two stages are optional for those who want their product to be glazed and decaled. There is almost always a demand by students to glaze their products, whereas there is less demand for decaling. It takes at least three weeks for an object to be cleaned, underglazed, and glazed. When the work (lessons) on the product is finished, the student can acquire it by reimbursing a certain amount of money to the teacher.

One can analyze what the elderly do at the ceramic calss from several points of view. First, they "work" there. What they do is not craftsmanship, since work is done on a piece, not the whole thing. It is similar to the work on a windshield in a car factory, rather than on the whole car. Alienation of labor is involved: one works on the object, but the finished product is not his unless he buys it. Second, the elderly do craftsmanship. They choose the product, its colors, and whether it should be glazed (and decaled). They also clean the products, underglaze, (and decal) them. The same type of product done by two students are different because of each person's special craftsmanship (creativity). The elderly (students) also put their initials in the back of the product to personalize it (something similar to the "**powder's mark**"). Third, what the elderly do is the imitation of work. None of the students learns how to make ceramics. What they do is simply cleaning and glazing ready-made products. They spend their "labor" on a ready-made object. The teacher does not pay them to do the work. On the contrary they, as students, have to pay to be in the class. They, as laborers of petty work, have to clean, underglaze, and glaze the products. And yet, they, as buyers, have to pay to own the product. There are two payments involved. One can argue that people buy the right to do some kind of productive work. This is similar to the parents' paying for their children's various classes: swimming, music, dance, etc. When the children perform before an audience, they do not get paid for their performances. However, the rationale for paying for children's classes cannot be used to explain old people's paying for classes. For children, the rationale is that they learn something, improve, and it is good for their future. But for the elderly, it is difficult to say that it is better for their future. The skill (if any) that they learn does not help them in later life. Thus, the payment for children's classes and those of the elderly may be structurally the same, but the purpose is different.

The paradox is that what is encompassed in all the above perspectives are combined. The students know that the **teacher** has made the products and they have done some petty work on them. The teacher is both knowledgeable of the art of ceramic making and the owner of means of production (i.e., the equipment). When asked why you cannot take the products home and work on them, the elderly answer: "We do not know how to do it. Besides, we do not have the equipment." On the other hand, they think **they** have made the products. When asked what the most interesting thing about the ceramic class is, they answer: "It is good to know that you did it yourself, with your own hands." Ironically, the elderly do not object to paying for what they say **they** have made. In addition to the fact that the students do not learn to make ceramics from scratch and they cannot make any products, even after working on several of them, their situation is different from a "work" place because they do not get paid for their labor. It is also different from "home" because there are payments involved, on the part of the elderly: one to be in the class, and one in order to acquire the product they have worked on. To distinguish "home" from "work," Schneider (1968:46) stresses love versus money. He writes:

> Home is not kept for money and, of those things related
> to home and family, it is said that there are some things

that money can't buy! The formula in regard to work is exactly reversed at home: What is done is done for love, not for money! And it is love, of course, that money can't buy.

"Love" is neither involved in the formation nor during the process of the ceramic classes. The senior citizens contract the formation of the classes by their fee. In fact, there will be no classes if the number of students is below a certain limit. Moreover, the finished product is not donated out of love as a gift to the senior citizens; they have to purchase what they themselves have helped producing.

Another example of playing the role of student while gaining little education and yet playing "work" is found in the activities of the elderly in the "rhythm band," composed of 10 to 20 persons who go to the Center once a week for one hour and play musical instruments. Two professional non-members, a pianist and a conductor (a music instructor), help the group activity. Once in a while, the rhythm band offers its service and takes trips to different nursing homes, Old Homes, children's rehabilitation centers, etc. Every year in December, the rhythm band plays in the December birthday party of the Center, which is also the Christmas party, and plays in some churches in town as well.

The Center furnishes the musical instruments for the rhythm band. Musical instruments consist of a piano, a drum, a set of bells (similar to xylophone), several tambourines, shakes, sticks, and triangles. The members of the rhythm band do not have to know how to read music. The only two persons who need to have a knowledge of music are the conductor and the pianist. They are the ones who have the note sheets in front of them. The rest of the group is supposed to look at the conductor and hit or shake his "musical instrument." The conductor conducts the group by both hitting her hands or saying, in slow or fast motions depending on the music, "hit hit," "one two three four." She also sometimes utters such meaningless sounds as "bum bum bim bim," or "dum dum dim dim."

Just as in the ceramic class, while it appears at first sight that the students (the elderly) play the music, there is a second reality in the whole process. Their exercise **is** and is **not** playing the music. Some of the musical instruments such as sticks look more like toys rather than musical instruments. Moreover, students do not learn musics at all. They can play as long as the conductor tells them "hit hit," "dim dim," etc. If she does not conduct them, they cannot play even the songs they have practiced more than twenty times. The only people who play the music are the professional musicians. They know the music. They also select the songs, as do the music teachers in schools.

Apart from the resemblance between the Center and schools, another example of similarity between pre-workers and post-workers can be seen in the way in which senior citizens are treated by the administrators of the Center. The administrators see the elderly as their children. They tell them what to do and what not to do. They simplify the language, rehearse and repeat what should be done several times. They also use various devices to please the members. In parties, they arrange the room in the most colorful manner. In games in which there are elements of winning and losing, the administrators mostly make use of the philosophy of "making everybody happy," and give prizes to everybody lest the losers feel sad by not getting a prize. The following examples illustrate these points.

As already mentioned, in monthly birthday parties, the executive director (or one of her employees in her absence) makes a speech and starts the program. Her speech covers announcements about the coming events (activities) of the Center, mentioning the sequence of getting the meal (a buffet style), and uttering the prayer. Those whose birthday is in that particular month get their lunch first, then those who are sitting at the table nearest to the kitchen and so forth. I have attended more than twenty-five birthday parties and have always observed the same sequence. However, each time the Administration finds it necessary to "instruct" the participants. Members do not seem to mind those repetitions. They do step by step what they are told to do. Each person usually thinks that he knows the sequence, but others do not know it. Insructions, repetitions, and simplifying the language are not limited only to birthday parties, but also used in other activites. When the Administration invites an entertainer, the staff may applaud the entertainer first and instruct (hint) everybody to clap. Speeches are uttered in a slow fashion containing repetitions. Children's talk is also prevalent. For instance, the title of one lecture in the "wellness series" was "Make mine milk" which means "prepare various kinds of food with milk for me." On one certain December birthday

106

party, also the Senior Center Christmas party, at the end of the activity, a non-member playing Santa Claus gave every person an orange as a gift. Before distributing the gift he greeted everybody very formally, but then he said jokingly: "I want you to behave yourselves in the coming new year. I have heard that some of you have not behaved yourselves." He, then, pointed at one of the ladies and said: "Joan, I have heard you have not behaved. Behave yourself, next year! O.K.?"

The Administration arranges the room for birthday parties and other special parties in a colorful manner. The room is always arranged before members arrive. White tablecloths, on which colorful papers are set lengthwise, cover the tables. In addition to napkins and silverware, there are vases of flowers and/or colorful candle holders on the tables. When these parties are in February, March, or December, and thus coinciding with Valentine's Day, St. Patrick's Day, or Christmas, such ritualistic colors as pink, green, and red dominate the room on walls, tables, and name tags. At birthday parties, those whose birthday falls in that particular month get a colorful tag (in the shape of a flower, butterfly, Santa Claus, etc.) on which it is written "Happy Birthday" to attach on their shirt.

Dominance of colors is also apparent in clothing. In annual dances for senior citizens, held by one of the charity organizations in town, organizers wear colorful clothes. Some wear clothes like clowns, paint their faces, have big colorful handkerchiefs in hand and seem eager to amuse the elderly by clowning and horseplay.

As guests, the elderly usually dress very formally. Men wear suits and ties. Women wear long or short evening dresses, have jewelry on, and wear lots of make-up. Some women constantly renew their lipstick after eating something. The organizers, on the other hand, wear unusual (acting) clothes, those of clowns, dancers, cowboys, etc. At one of these annual dances, one of the organizers (a girl) was wearing a leotard and a pair of tights on which there were holes which showed her body. Some had masks on. Some men were wearing women's clothes. One of them had a pair of tights, sneakers, and a short blouse under which he (she) had some cloths as his (her) breasts. The behavior of the two groups are also very distinct. While the elderly behave solemnly and formally, the organizers do funny things, hop, or walk and dance in a strange manner to make the party look fun and full of excitement. The annual dance looks more like a show, which includes refreshments, rather than a party in which hosts and guests unite as one group.[8] The hosts (i,e., the organizers of annual dances) assume the role of entertainers, and the guests (i.e., the elderly) assume the role of entertainees.

The Senior Center administrators, and others who serve the elderly, give away prizes on many occasions. These prizes also represent another aspect of the structural similarity between pre-workers and post-workers. Prizes are distributed at bingo, at annual dances, and at some of the Center birthday parties.[9] At the Center, there is a one hour of playing bingo on Fridays. Various prizes are set aside for the winners.[10] Food stuffs (snacks, sauces, pickles), and cosmetics (lipsticks, eye shadows) comprise the prizes. Each round, when a person wins he can choose the prize he wants. Those who win more than once, and thus get more than one prize, are greeted by such comments as "It is your day today!" "You are taking all the prizes!" "You are lucky today!"[11] In spite of those comments, however, losing does not mean that one goes home empty-handed. In the end of the game, everybody is asked to take a prize home. Therefore, anybody who plays bingo takes a prize home regardless of winning or losing, winning only means that one gets more prizes.[12] The point is that senior citizens do not have to do something extraordinary to be eligible to get a prize. The idea of "making everybody happy" dominates the process of prize giving.[13] The following examples will clarify the point further.

Take the prizes given to the elderly at the annual dance. When guests (i.e., the elderly) arrive, they are given a numbered ticket which makes them eligible for a prize. As the program starts, people are asked to go to the refreshment table and help themselves. Refreshments include beverages, small sandwiches, cakes, cookies, cheeses and crackers, and sometimes colorful cotton candies made at the party. When almost everybody has helped himself, people are invited to dance (either by themselves, with their partners, or with the organizers), and various prizes are distributed in different forms.

The "cake walk" is one of the ways through which the elderly become eligible for a prize. Every forty-five minutes, the organizers tie a long rope, on which many numbers are attached, to four chairs in the middle of the ballroom. While the music is being played, guests are supposed to dance around the rope. When the music stops people should hold one of the numbers on the rope in front of them. They are also asked not to "cheat" (i.e., not to hold more than one number). One of the organizers, who stands in the middle of the circle (or square) and holds a sack full of numbers in it, takes one number out as soon as the music stops, and reads it loudly. The person who holds that number on the rope is the winner and wins a cake, a sack of cookies, or a loaf of fruit bread. (Prizes are usually donated by some stores in town). The "cake walk" lasts half an hour during which five or six persons win. After one round, the organizers take the rope and bring it back forty-five minutes later. The "cake walk" is performed three or four times each night in which about twenty persons win prizes.

The "age dance" is another way of getting prizes at the annual dance. Again, the guests (senior citizens) are asked to dance in a circle. After a couple of minutes the music stops and one of the organizers asks those younger than sixty-five to leave the circle. He also wants people to be "honest" about their age.[14] This process of elimination continues until only the oldest male and female remain. Each gets a prize (a rose or an orchid). Similar to the "Cake walk," there is no effort involved by the winner to win, here age alone being the determinant.

Yet another way of getting prizes is through "having a sticker under one's chair." The organizers stick a piece of colorful paper on the underside of some of the chairs (about ten of them) before the senior citizens arrive. Some time in the middle of the party, an organizer asks people to look under their chair. Those who find the sticker get a prize (cakes, cookies, bouquets of flowers donated by some stores in town). The last way of getting a prize is "having the numbered ticket," given to the elderly upon their arrival. Close to the end of the party, the organizers draw eight to ten winning numbers, the owner of each gets a prize. In all cases, getting a prize depends on chance rather than one's special effort in doing something.[15]

At both annual dances and special monthly birthday parties (such as the one which coincides with the Christmas party of the Center), out of 150 to 200 persons, at most 50 of them win a prize. The rest do not get any prize at all. In these cases, however, there is usually a sack of "favors" (goodies) for each person on the tables. Each sack of favors includes some of the following items: a deck of playing cards, pens or pencils, telephone pads, small mirrors, cosmetics, shaving creams, an advertizing magnet, etc. At annual dances, the charity organization offers a potted plant or a box of "animal crackers" in addition to a date book. One year, at the dance, I expressed my astonishment with the shape of the "animal crackers" to one of my informants. He said: "Haven't you ever seen them? 'Animal crackers' are used a lot in kindergartens." In further inquiry, I realized that "animal crackers" have a special significance in American culture. I was informed that, Generally speaking, an American child waits for his mother to come back from shopping hoping that she would bring "animal crackers." The cookies (crackers) are specially used in soups (for children). "Animal crackers" are associated with mothers (a very important character in American culture), not necessarily with kindergartens. In terms of getting prizes, both annual dances and monthly birthday parties function like weekly bingo playings: nobody is a loser; everybody takes something home.

The idea of "making everybody happy" is also prevalent in parties for children. Take the children's birthday parties, the mother of the birthday person usually prepares small gifts in wrapping papers to give to the children who bring presents for her own child because children cannot emotionally afford not getting presents. Thus, the children who go to a birthday party carrying a gift along do not usually leave empty-handed. The games played at children's parties are not structurally different from the games played at the parties for the elderly. Winnings are mostly based on the person's luck rather than his effort. Music is used as an element to help winning (or losing), especially in two of the most common games: sitting on a chair and holding an apple. In these games, when the music stops the person who is not sitting on a chair, and the one who holds the apple are losers.

The elderly themselves sometimes explicitly say that they are returning to their "second childhood." The comparison between the two opposite age-grades: children and senior citizens, with regard to their activities (i.e., pre-working and post-working) demonstrates yet another dimension of "work" (or playing work) in American culture. The similarity between the Senior Center and schools, and the similarity between the way in which senior citizens and children are treated indicate an imitation of "work" dominant in the activities of the elderly.[16] What makes it significant is the degree to which playing ("make-believe"), as opposed to work, is present. However, as mentioned before, there are structural similarities between the activities of children and senior citizens but the content is different.

Schooling and classes are a way of socializing the children for entering the sphere of work. The children are less of "persons" in the sense of being "self-sufficient autonomous individuals." Insofar as work and productivity are concerned, it is normal if they are "undifferentiated" individuals. They have the "future" ahead of them. By providing for children's education, the society actually protects its own longevity. Moreover, the children learn to seek identity, in order to become "persons" (as Barnett and Silverman define) in American culture. The same cannot be said of the elderly. Both individually and socially they have already experienced the life of "differentiated individuals." After retirement, they are not being socialized to enter the sphere of work. They do not have a long "productive" future ahead of them, either. Their identity as complete "persons" is undermined by their exclusion from the work sphere. How they react to this new situation is conditioned by the cultural values of the society. But, what do they do? Their options and the way in which they continue their identity as complete "persons" will be the focus of the next section.

(B). The notion of production

Over 5000 Senior Centers, and a good number of nursing homes, and residential places, etc., provide services for the elderly in the United States. They perform an important function in satisfying many of the material needs of the elderly. But they also function as social institutions by offering activities for their clients. The elderly participate in those activities to enjoy themselves, stay busy, and more importantly "improve" themselves and/or "help" the community by their volunteer work. It is this aspect of their function that this section is concerned with. The elderly take numerous "beginning" classes: German, Spanish, French, painting, ceramics, crafts, and so forth. They also continue to do what they used to do as crafters, painters, bridge players, etc. Some start totally new tasks as volunteers in hospitals and various charity organizations, or join some national or local associations. When I began the fieldwork, one of the first question I asked was: why do the elderly have to make the extra effort of going to a place such as the senior center to do exercise, paint, sew, read Bible, or do similar functions? One important way to find the answer, I discovered, was to find out what the elderly gain in those activities. To ask the

111

question differently, what do they "produce?" By the term "produce," I am referring to the "socially determined individual production" (Marx 1973). The distinction between individual and society is especially important in the context of American culture which is considered to be, ideologically speaking, "individualistic." Louis Dumont (1965, 1970) distinguishes between what he calls a holistic society and an individualistic one.

> In the first case, the main value emphasis and reference is on order, tradition, orientation of each particular human being to the ends prescribed for the society. In the second, the main reference is to the attributes, claims, or welfare of each individual human being irrespective of his place in society. In the first case, man is considered essentially as a social being, deriving his very humanity from the society as a whole (universitas) of which he is a part; in the second, each man as an individum of the species is a substance existing by itself and there is a tendency to reduce, to obscure, or to suppress the social aspect of his nature (Dumont 1970:32).

Whereas it is difficult to divide societies so rigidly into totally holistic or totally individualistic, students of American culture have a consensus in calling the American society as an individualistic one (Vogt 1950; Barnett and Silverman 1979; Schneider 1968). Individualism and protecting one's own interest (independent of the society) are prevalent at the Senior Center too. The elderly do not participate in the activity of the Center in order to satisfy the quota requirement of the Center to get funded. By doing so, however, they help the Center keep itself in operation, even though this is not their reason to join the Center. The role of the Center is similar to a salesperson or a matchmaker. As a salesperson, the Center sells its commodity (i.e., activities) to the members. The more the members buy the commodity (i.e., participate in the activities) the more the Center gets funded. As a matchmaker, the Center tries to find out about the interests of the members and, by offering the activities, match a person with the right kind of activity. To inform each member of what exists, the Center advertizes the activities in various forms and occasions: monthly newsletter, birthday parties, and

112

quarterly parties held for the purpose of orientation of new members. Moreover, the Center has to cancel the activities in which there is no interest and/or enough attendance (at least eight persons). On this level, the Center needs the members in order to function and to get funded. On another level, the members need the Center (more on this later). In other words, the members and the Center are symbiotically related.

As mentioned above, the members value their own interest more than those of the Center (i.e., the society). One major interest, in keeping with American cultural value, is to emphasize one's individuality. By becoming "president," "secretary," and so forth of the various activities provided by the Center, the elderly distinguish themselves from others and create a sense of identity.

In American society, distinguishing oneself from others ("differentiation") is best symbolized through one's "work;" one has social recognition through what he does. According to O'Toole *et al* (1978:6).

> Work [in the United States] is a powerful force in shaping a person's sense of identity. We find that most, if not all, working people tend to describe themselves in terms of the work group or organizations to which they belong. The question, 'who are you?' often solicits an organizationally related response, such as 'I work for IBM,' or 'I'm a Stanford professor.' Occupational role is usually a part of this response for all classes: 'I'm a steelworker,' or 'I'm a lawyer.' In short: **people tend to become what they do.**' (Emphases added).

If "people tend to become what they do," as O'Toole *et al.* argue, what is the situation of pre-workers and post-workers (children and the elderly respectively)? Both children and retirees are undifferentiated as "work" is concerned. Children prepare themselves for being differentiated by education (learning different skills) so that in adulthood they are recognized as independent individuals. As they grow, they become more differentiated. The differentiation reaches its peak at adulthood. In the "public" sphere, one has a social recognition as a mechanic, lawyer, nurse, teacher, etc., not, for example, as a person who likes certain colors, movies, or flowers (unless they are used professionally). The society recognizes a person not only through what he does but also through where he does it (i.e., in what organization). "Corporate individual" and "organizational man" seem to be appropriate characterizations: a sharp deviation from the family enterprise system which dominated early American life. Unlike that time when self-employed people were proud of their independence and achievement, Paul Dickson (1971) captures the traumatic experience of those who are treated almost as failures when introduce themselves as the self-employed.

> No less dramatic...are those questions of identity which present themselves to the self-employed. These identity crises and situations usually come packaged in little episodes which occur when others find that they have encountered a bona fide weirdo without a boss.... You are stopped by a traffic policeman to be given a ticket and he asks the name of your employer and you say that you work for yourself. Next he asks, 'Come on, where do you work? Are you employed or not?' You say, 'Self-employed.'... He, among others you meet, knows that self-employment is a tried euphemism for being out of work.... You become extremely nervous about meeting new people because of the ever-present question, 'Who are you with?' When your answer fails to attach you to a recognized organization...both parties to the conversation often become embarrassed by your obscurity.

In scholarly journals, writers specify their names and profession or the institution they belong to rather than their name and their favorite color, food, etc. Writers with no affiliation try to forge it by the usage of the adjective "free-lance." When people grow old, the retirement excludes them from both the profession and the organization. Retirement abruptly makes a differentiated individual undifferentiated. A retiree may take pride in previously being a physician, executive, nurse, etc., but what matters is that he/she is now retired, like any other retiree. According to Charles Winick (1964):

> Inasmuch as work has such a profound role in establishing a person's life space, emotional tone, family

114

situation, object relations, and where and how he will live, either the absense of work or participation in marginal work often makes it likely that he will develop a pervasive **atonie**. (Original emphasis).

By the usage of the term "atonie" Winick refers to a condition of deracination--a feeling of rootlessness, lifelessness, and dissociation-- a word which in the original Greek meant a string that does not vibrate, that has lost its vitality. Besides, like it does among the Nuer (Evans-Pritchard 1940), another egalitarian society, work helps regulate one's basic rhythms and cyclical patterns of day, week, month, and year. Without work, time patterns become confused.

In order to cope with the problem of undifferentiation, the retired elderly try to do something to become different from all other retirees. The Senior Center is a means to achieve this goal. It is an organization with which members can associate. On outdoor functions or travels the participants make a conscious effort to display their affinity with the Center. For example, they may wear a badge with their name along with the name of the Center. They participate as sellers or representatives of the Center in annual bazaars, parades, and in their relationship with other organizations. The Center both encourages and provides opportunities for its members to project their distinctiveness. At monthly birthday parties and some other activities, the Center provides name tags for the members. It is true that name tags mostly symbolize that a person has paid for the meal, but the Center provides special colorful tags for the birthday people to differentiate them from other participants. Moreover, although no activity is meant to be a "one man show," people try to create their own show as good crafters, bridge players, hard working puppet makers, etc. Some even try to get recognition through wearing a special type of clothing. For example, Fran wears big hats which usually match her dresses. After introducing herself, she usually mentions that everybody calls her "the lady in big hats." Ethel always wears purple clothes. She also mentions that people know her as "the lady in purple."

Some people insist on attaching name tags on their shirts in all activities. They say: "People will know who we are if we wear name tags." Some senior citizens are very particular about how and where to attach the tag. When I first started the fieldwork, I was not aware of the significance of those tags. For a while I wore mine on the left side of my shirt, but I was instructed by Irene and Ruth to wear it on the right side. They gave the following reason: "when people shake hands with you, it is easier for them to look at the right side of your shirt. That way people do not have to turn their face to see your name." In the application forms that members had filled out to join the Center, in response to the following question: "In your own words describe how you would want the Center to best serve our Senior Community" some had answered: "by making us wear a badge with our name on it." These people had not explained how wearing name tags could help the Center to best serve the Senior Community. Some members have expressed to me their dissatisfaction with the Center because it does not give them a permanent name tag after they join the Center. The name tags, thus, mean and symbolize a lot more than introducing the person's name. They symbolize and externalize the person's identity in terms of his association with an organization. They differentiate a person from all other members and from all other elderly. People also insist on signing their name on the attendance sheets for each activity group. Often the members themselves are more concerned about signing the sheet than the Administration.

Some others find the identity through assuming a special position in the respective activity, a chairperson, co-chairperson, representative, secretary, and/or treasure. Some of these positions rotate so that most people get a chance to act in those capacities. Still, others find identity in simply participating in the activities. They justify their participation on the basis of "work." For instance, members of the craft activity group have said to me that it is good "to work with one's hands." They consider a satisfying old age an active one, and a non-active old age and uninvolvement as vegetation. "One rots if one is not active," they say. One of my informants said the following about her non-active mother: "It was easier to bury her than visit."

What does the preoccupation with activities mean in terms of what the members "produce." Using Marx's categories, the membership at the Center resembles more a system of producing 'exchange-value' than that of producing 'use-value'. Its broad objective is not the reproduction of the individual's place in the group, but his transformation. The individual is transformed from an undifferentiated retiree to a differentiated bowling player, president of the men's club, the United Way envelope stuffer,

German learner, traveller, etc. All these roles re-generate self-identity for the retiree. Marx's "commodity" in this case is the individual's self-identity.

I have already mentioned about one side of the paradox that exists in the relationship between the Center and its members (i.e., the dependency of the Center on members for having more membership and more attendance in order to get funded and function as an organization). In this sense, the Center sells its commodity (i.e., activities) to senior citizens. Senior citizens also depend on the Center for it helps them re-generate "self-identity." Drawing on Marx's analysis of capitalist system, and the anthropological literature (e.g., Bohannan 1955; Levi-Strauss 1969), one can argue that every social formation consists of a combination of hierarchically ordered relationships (see Godelier 1975; Gregory 1981). In capitalism, for instance, the sphere of wage labor (c-m-c', i.e., commodity-money-a qualitatively different type of commodity) is dominated by industrial capital (m-c-m', i.e., money-commodity-quantitatively different money) which is in turn dominated by financial capital (m-m',i.e., money-more money). The participation of the members at the Senior Center is not capitalism. What exist are similar processes, although there is no financial capital (i.e., m-m').

Through participating in the activities, the members at the Senior Center produce self-identity (activity-self-identity-more activity, i.e., a-s-a'). This process, then, results in producing more self-identity and participating in more activities (self- identity-activity-more self-identity, i.e., s-a-s'), hence the repetition of the cycle. When a person is known and admired as an active one, he/she feels necessary to participate in more activities. As one very active member of the Center commented: "At the Center, there are three types of people: those who make things happen, those who watch things happen, and those who do not know what is happening." By saying this, not only was he putting a lower value on those "who do not know what is happening," but also was boasting himself as a person who "makes things happen."

I sometimes explained to the people that the elderly in other societies do not have Senior Centers and the elderly are occupied with family and ritualistic functions. I would then ask people whether they consider themselves more privileged or less than senior citizens in other societies. Most of them would consider themselves more privileged than senior citizens in other societies. Some argue that: "We are more privileged than others because of the Senior Center. It gives us more life of our own. It gives us more self-confidence. It helps us be more visible."

Following retirement, "Identity" is what a lot of people feel they lose most. One of my informants described his situation after an early retirement as follows:

> I thought I didn't have identity if I didn't have a job. It took me thirteen years to accept retirement. I felt cheated. I missed my job. I had no life except work. I changed six jobs after I was retired.

This statement, uttered with bitterness can be compared with the years which takes one to finish elementary and high school; it takes shorter for an illiterate to educate himself than for this person to cope with retirement.

As mentioned in chapter one, I voluntarily offered a humanities course at the Center entitled **Work and life** in which the participants and I discussed various issues about work and their influence on our lives in the context of the readings. One of the readings was an excerpt from Sholom Aleichem's story entitled "Mr. Green has a job." The theme of the story is a discussion of the problems immigrants face in their new country. Not only are they forced to learn a new language and adjust to a new culture, but they frequently learn that their adopted country, more often than not, has no need for many of their skills which were highly valued in their homeland. Doing odd jobs, thus, seems to be their fate. For example, Aleichem's story of Mr. Green (called Greenberg back home) is typical. In America, Mr. Green finally finds a job blowing **shofar** (ram's horn) in a **shul** (synagogue) on the High Holy Days. Making the use of the story, I asked the participants (the members who had taken the course) the following question: "Can comparison be made between immigrants finding their way in a new land and older people experiencing the new land of retirement?" Almost all students agreed. Some commented: "Retirement is very difficult. You don't know the rules. You ask all sorts of questions: 'How do I fit into a new society?', 'How do I fill my time?'"

Identity is so attached to "work" or "just doing something" that many of the informants believed "the person who has the most difficulty retiring is the one who doesn't have an outside interest." When asked what "outside interest" means, members referred to some kind of activity and/or involvement in national and international affairs. Some did not find even sickness as an excuse for non-involvement. They said: "in that case, one has to be involved through newspapers and television." They explained that these "involvements rejuvenate one's energy. They are similar to recharging one's battery."

Ironically, television was considered a means to provide idleness for many informants. As one said: "Television and rocking chair should be banished. T.V. is addictive." In further inquiry, he said that there is nothing wrong with television per se, but how one uses it. The recommended way of using a television was watching the news for the purpose of being involved. The rocking chair was also considered to be addictive. Some members made extra effort to bring this "fact" to the attention of others. At one birthday party (September 1985), Hazel who turned 99 in September, was introduced and interviewed (as an achiever). She saw the meaning of life in being active, getting up in the morning with the desire that "there is a day full of hard work ahead of you."[17] In between the audience's applause, she mentioned some of her activities: gardening, travelling, going to the Senior Center, church activities, and housework. As regards the latter, she sarcastically said: "When people come to my house I tell them that if they find any dust in the house please write their name and telephone number on the dust so that I can call them later." What she hated most was a rocking chair. She advised people "not to sit on rocking chairs because they will get 'rocking chair humps' on their back." She also advised people "to use their mind. It won't get flabby." The point is not the cleanliness of Hazel who does not let her house to get dusty. The point is the obsession of the elderly with being active. They constanly admire themselves or other elderly for being active.

The social side of being active (i.e., the society's approval) is extremely important for senior citizens. One informant said: "People would say 'poor thing' if one is not active. One is more successful when one is active." Other comments, concerning the society's approval, are as follows: "The way I see myself is by the way I think I am seen by other people," "My view of myself is a reflection of other people's view." "People tell me that I do good work, and I need that."[18] A volunteer justified her volunteering as "it helps me feel needed." Note the latter's comment. The retirees who feel they are no longer needed outside the Center make a conscious effort to be needed inside the Center. The inside/outside opposition is significant in this case. While one feels just a retiree ('nobody,' as some put it) outside the Center, one feels needed ('somebody') inside the Center. Note the roles people take. They are presidents, vice-presidents, or treasurers of different kinds of clubs and committees such as the cheer committee, men's club, bridge club, newsletter committee, etc. In business corporations or government offices, these roles are important positions (and include many responsibilities).

I discussed the issue of volunteer work to many of those who were volunteers themselves. I asked them why they do volunteer work. Some answered: "Volunteer work gives illusion of work. One feels important by doing something," or "having something definite, some routine work is important." I mentioned to the elderly that volunteer work is beneficial to the organization, and that some organizations (e.g., hospitals) could not as easily function if there were no volunteers. I asked the people whether they feel that the organizations exploit volunteers. Everybody answered that " organizations do not exploit volunteers." People also disagreed with me that volunteer work is beneficial to the organization. They argued that "volunteer work is beneficial for the people. It is nice that the organizations let people (especially the elderly) to voluntarily work for them."

Whether assuming various roles or performing volunteer work, members do their best to keep themselves busy, and in many cases, to be more significant than others. Thus, as much as the Senior Center needs the people as members, the members need the Center (or any place where they can "do" something) to produce self-identity in order to re-become the kind of differentiated persons they once were in the work place. Do they really become like the people in the work sphere? Is there anything which stops retired elderly from that? I shall discuss these questions in the next section.

C. Age-consciousness: the paradox

The "age" of the elderly seems to be the factor which, the elderly think, stops them from becoming like the people in the sphere of work. When I first began the fieldwork, the executive director of the Senior Center advised me not to ask the informants two culturally tabooed questions: age and income. I, then, was prepared to forget about the passage of time and the age of my informants (who were all above fifty-five years of age). To my surprise, it took me no more than a week to find out that the members of the Center are extremely conscious of their age, the age of other people, and the passage of time. While referring to themselves or others, the elderly classify everybody by "age" more than any other category such as social class, religion, nationality, ethnicity, etc. Speeches are thick with references to age (and its associates such as well-being and illness). At the Center, one frequently hears such phrases and terms as we old folks, senior citizens, old times, old timers, old days, youngsters, young lady (or gentleman), children, kids, etc. The age of those members who are considered very old (ninety-nine years for example) are often announced, at the Senior Center. Those people are introduced and applauded at birthday parties. Talking about deaths and sicknesses take place frequently on a one to one basis in form of gossip or asking someone about another person's condition. The Administration announces deaths in the monthly newsletter, but never publicly at the podium, in birthday parties.[19]

At the time of doing fieldwork, I was a generation or two younger than my informants. This raised many comments on my age (and what I was doing there). In fact, all the people who first encountered me at the Center would first tell me: "This is a Senior Center. You don't belong here, what do you do?" Or "You don't look like being eligible to be a member. I would be disillusioned if you were a member. I would ask you the secret for staying so young." At the beginning, such comments appeared as a mild objection to my presence at the Center. It seemed that people did not want an outsider (e.g., a younger person) to enter their domain. This attitude changed later on when most people got to know me. I was no longer considered to be a threat. Only the newcomers would express their astonishment about my presence.

With regard to what I was doing as an anthropologist, many people thought I was specialized in archeology. As one informant said: "Are you studying anthropology? Instead of digging you should study us. Some of us have been dead for so long. We are just not buried yet." Others simply joked about it. For instance, in a cruise orientation (held for those who were going on a cruise) one man asked me: "Are you here to see how excited the old folks are?" Another person said: "She is here to see what we old folks do." Stressing "oldness" was not only projected in people's relationship with me. People sometimes wondered as to why the younger staff at the Senior Center worked there. Once someone commented about the young people who work for the Senior Center the following: "They must enjoy old people. This is why they work here."[20]

The extreme age-consciousness, among the elderly, can be viewed in almost everything: in the way in which they decide about various issues, in their relationships, in their talking about the past or future, and in their concerns about what they eat or how they find the direction to a place, etc. People's major decisions depend very much upon their awareness of their "old" age. Take the case of Carmen, for example. After retirement, Carmen moved into this State to be near her daughter who is married and has two children. Carmen, then, joined the Senior Center and decided to voluntarily work in the kitchen preparing the lunch. After several years, Carmen's daughter had to move to another State. Carmen, who moved here to be near her daughter, did not move with her daughter. She argued:

> I am old. I have to start all over again. Moving is good for young people. They can easily get to know new people and make friends. But for old people it is not easy. Now, I know some people at the Center. I come here everyday. I do what I like to do (i.e., working at the kitchen). Life would be dull for me in another place.

In another case, a couple who sold their house in a large city and moved here argued that: "This town is good for old people. It doesn't have pollution." Many people sell their houses and buy an apartment or rent a smaller place because they think they are "too old to take care of the garden."

In their relationship with others, the elderly take their old age into consideration. As one woman talked about her conversation with her son, she said: "My son says that 'I talk too much and I snore.' I say: 'Old people fall apart.'" While talking about various issues, the elderly reflect a strong sense of comparison which has something to do with aging or the passage of time. They are concerned about other people's age, and the difference between old times and now. They compare the prices, how much they made, say, as a "fourteen year old boy in 1916," etc. They compare their abilities with those of others. For instance, one man told me: "As a young person you have a certain amount of energy to spend. I don't have that body of energy." They mention their age difference among themselves. Such comments are frequent: "since you are the youngest of us...," "I don't remember that. I was a kid, then," "You were not born yet," "What did you do as a young man (or woman)," "I don't know about the tornadoes in 1922. That was before my time." Prices and inflation are interesting topics for the elderly. They compare the movie theatre tickets, gasoline prices, etc. When the elderly talk about the future, there is a feeling of doubt or sadness in their speech. For instance, one elderly once said: "I don't think I will ever get to go to space. I am not that age (i.e., young)."

The elderly are conscious of their old age in everyday matters. Driving, for instance, is not an easy task for many old people. They may have poor eyesight. Many of them do not want to drive at night, especially if they do not know the direction. During Christmas, the rhythm band at the Center is sometimes invited to play music in some churches in town. If the program is scheduled for the evening, those who drive and do not know the direction usually drive to the place once in the day time (to learn the direction before the actual time. (Thus, they do one task twice)). Food is one of the categories in which the elderly are very conscious of. One constantly hears comments on the types of food which are good or bad for the elderly. For example: "Pickles are not good for us at our age. They have too much salt," "We don't eat eggs more than once every week or two. Eggs have cholestrol and are not good for old people, it is said," "I don't make pies. I buy them from store. But I just eat the fruit not the crust. It is not good for people at my age."

As already mentioned, the executive director of the Center requested me not to discuss the issue of age with the informants, specifically not to ask their age. Ironically, the Administration and those who deal with the elderly project the oldness of the people in many different forms even though they may not directly ask each one of them how old they are. In other words, while there is a verbal taboo on inquiring about age, it is constantly expressed in non-verbal manners. Whereas some activities at the Senior Center are general and can be of interest to anybody, many of the activities are meant to be especially for older people. Such programs as Wellness Series, Oral Histories, Mature/alive Drivers Course, Dental Education, Pure Gold Aerobics, Sittercise, Armchair Massage, Arthritis Club, Heart Saver Course, Diet Workshop, Grandparents Ice Cream Social, and the Elders' Club are some of these activities. In addition, people's birthdays are celebrated once a month, and those born in that month wear a name tag and an extra tag on which it is written happy birthday (expressing their getting older). If someone is considered very old, he/she is introduced, interviewed, and applauded at the birthday party.

The volunteers (non-members), at the Center, also project the oldness of the elderly by different means. The conductor of the rhythm band, a woman in her thirties, usually selects old songs of 1920s or 1930s for the activity group to play. She often asks the music players whether they remember such-and-such songs. In performances, she comments on the oldness or newness of the songs, and if the audience is elderly (in a nursing home for example) she asks them whether they remember such-and-such old song. She sometimes introduces the band members to the audience. She does not forget to introduce the oldest person and the "baby" (i.e., the youngest person) in the band. The lecturer in the Wellness Series also projects the oldness of the elderly and speaks about how an old person can take care of himself. She, once, discussed the value of calcium or milk in the elderly's diet to prevent many diseases, particularly osteoporosis. She defined the disease as "a thinning and weakening of bone structures on a downhill situation (i.e, old age) for women at age forty and for men after sixty." It seemed ironic that the lecturer of the wellness series used the phrase "downhill situation" in front of the elderly. I have already mentioned that at the annual dances, held by a charity organization in town, the senior citizens are invited to the "age dance" in which the oldest guests (one man and one woman) are recognized as the winners of the dance. During the dance, the speaker (one of the organizers) mentions various ages and asks those younger than the age mentioned to leave the circle. He also requests people, several times, not to "cheat" about their age.[21]

An old age homogeneous society such as the Senior Center blurs cultural categories of aging. The members' extreme age-consciousness results in a paradox. It separates them from the rest of the society, and simultaneously unites them with the rest of the society. On the one hand, a glorification of old age exists. People get together at the Center to celebrate this glory. On the other hand, a devaluation of old age is visible. People get together at the Center to prove that they are like everybody else in the society (as productive, active, and attractive). The rest of this section will clarify these points.

(1) Age glorification

On the level of the glorification of old age, the elderly hold that old age generates its own value. They try to raise the (low?) status of the elderly and create a myth about themselves. The usage of such terms as "golden age," "silver-haired," "senior citizens" offers an old age identity, and reinforces the separateness of older persons as one set apart from those who are not old. Those terms also offer a more precious value for aging as gold and silver, and a higher place for the elderly as being senior. These terms and phrases are used by both the society as a whole, and the elderly in particular. In some cases, however, the elderly call themselves "old folks" but they seem to be offended if someone addresses them as old folks. They prefer to be called senior citizens. I discussed these terms with some of my informants. I mentioned that some organizations dealing with senior citizens are planning to change the phrase 'senior citizens' to 'older Americans.' I asked the elderly whether they would have any objections to the new phrase.

My informants and I, first, discussed the connotations of the phrases 'senior citizen' and 'older American.' Whereas the phrase 'senior citizen' represents a higher status for the person, it separates him from the rest of the society. The phrase is segregationist. It puts the elderly in one category in which they must remain. The phrase 'older American,' on the other hand, compares one American with other Americans in terms of age. This phrase does not show a higher status for the person. Neither does it separate the person from the rest of the society. My informants expressed no preference for the usage of any of these phrases. Actually one of them said: "The change of the phrase senior citizen to older American will soon mean the same as senior citizen to people." By that, she meant the phrase 'older American' would also be segregationist after a while.

There is a national organization serving senior citizens which is called the "Gray Panthers." I once called the organization and asked them about the reason behind such a name. I was told that the term 'Gray' stands for the gray hair of the elderly and the term 'panthers' shows that although the elderly are old and have gray hair they are as strong as panthers. A half-hour show on television about four older women living in Florida is called the "Golden Girls." At the Senior Center, the usage of the terms in which there is an implicit high status is frequent. The aerobics course is referred to as the "pure gold aerobics," and the driving course is referred to as the "alive/mature drivers course."

In some cases, the age-consciousness and the glorification of old age lead to an emphasis on the elderly's distinctiveness not only from the rest of the society, but also from other older people. There is an "Elders' Club" at the Senior Center which consists of those who have been the members of the Center for more than eight years. The club is an age-segregated group within a society (i.e., the Senior Center) which is already age-segregated.[22]

Another aspect of the glorification of old age is apparent in the elderly's presenting themselves as skilled craftspersons and as historians. The elderly demonstrate their valuable art skills by operating various bazaars (with the help of the Senior Center) and selling artifacts or home-made pastries.[23] The elderly approach the status of being historians through an activity called "Oral History," held once a week at the Center from September to May. As mentioned before, the oral history group consists of about twenty persons. The activity group has projects to cover, and assignments for each person. Depending on the age of the members, the time period for each project is from 1890s to the present. People should take advantage of their memories and talk about the past. However, some people do research on their particular topic (assignment). With the help of the Senior Center as a mediator, the oral history group offers its service (i.e., speaking about life in the past) to schools and educational organizations in town and nearby cities. I took several trips with the oral history group to those schools. In one of those trips (November 1983, W. middle school), on the way to school one of the members said:

> We (the elderly) have something which is unique. We
> have not only read about cars or airplanes in books, but

also have seen their developments. We grew up with them. We should contribute our experience to those kids in schools.

If somebody in the group does not feel confident enough others try to encourage him. Once a woman expressed her uneasiness about going to school and said: "I don't have anything to say." Everybody objected to her and said: "Whatever you say is interesting." In one of the classes, one of the elderly asked students whether they had grandparents. After some students raised their hands indicating a positive answer, the old person advised them to talk to their grandparents. He said:

When I was a kid I had one grandfather, but I didn't talk to him much. I regret it now. Talk to your grandparents. Ask them about their lives. They have a lot to offer. You will learn a lot from them.

When the elderly go to schools as oral historians, they say that they want to show two things: 1-Life did not use to be as easy as it is today in terms of technology and facilities. 2-They still had fun: talked to people, made friends, enjoyed themselves. They also want to, as they say, "impress children that things have changed." To express the difficulties of the past, the elderly take any opportunity to talk about them. For instance, they emphasize that there were not many electrical gadgets, or since fabrics were not permanent press people spent a lot of their time ironing. The elderly often speak about the difficulties of going to school in old times. They say:

We had to walk to school two miles a day, going back and forth. There was no school bus. There was no cafeteria in schools. We walked home for lunch. The principal would punish us if we were late. We had a lot of homework to do.

Whereas speaking about the difficulties of the past gives the elderly a sense of "achievement and success" which helps them be recognized as those who "have made it," it does not stop them to remind the audience that they had fun in spite of the hard times. The elderly do not hesitate to glorify old times. The followings are some quotations of what they say about the past. "People were happier in old times." "In old times, there were no ready made toys for children. Children used their imagination. They used whatever they found instead of fancy things. For example, they used rocks to draw hopscotch rather than a chalk." "There was no teen age pregnancy (out of marriage) in old times." "Christmas was not commercial (therefore better). Christmas trees were decorated not fancy like now but with more feelings."

Glorification of age and old times gives the elderly a feeling of resentment towards the present time and the younger generation. They attribute evil to the younger generation.[24] The elderly are the "good guys" and the younger generation are the "bad guys." The "Bible Study" activity group always prays for young people "to behave themselves." The elderly disapprove of many aspects of the behavior of the younger generation, namely the living together of unmarried boys and girls. A person who usually rents her apartment to young students once said that she never rents her apartment to an unmarried couple. Others agreed with her that unmarried girls are not supposed to live with boys. They, then, criticized those who rent a place to such couples. They said: "Those landlords care only about money." The elderly use such terms as "real headache" to refer to teen-agers because they make so much noise and play music loudly. They also think that young people do not care what they eat, and that they eat to just fill the stomach. The elderly often complain about their grandchildren's misbehavior. The elderly consider the today's parents responsible for juvenile delinquency, because they are less disciplined and put less pressure on their children, compared to old timers.

The elderly value old times and older generation highly. I discussed many different issues with the elderly and asked their opinions. They had a strong sense of comparison between old and new, young and old. When asked about work and "work ethic," the elderly think that work ethic is disappearing in American culture. One elderly commented:

> Pride of workmanship is gone. My generation was
> worried about it. People were conscious of work.
> There are two kinds of income: psychic and material.
> My generation asked for psychic income. I enjoyed my

work so much that it was a shame to get paid. Now, people ask for material income.

When asked why cowboy movies are so appealing to Americans, the elderly replied:

> Movie going population is young. Young people don't value the family. They would like to get away from family. They like to be free like cowboys, dependent on nobody and nowhere. Motor cycle movies are also appealing because of young people.

When I told a group of my informants about Thomas Jefferson and that he did not want the University of Virginia to have a president and wanted it to have a rotating headmanship of one year among every faculty member, one old gentleman said: "Jefferson was, at that time, eighty-two and probably out-of-touch with twenty year olds." Everybody else in the group smiled and nodded. The group was very pleased to find out that the rotating idea did not endure after Jefferson's death because students created so many problems. The elderly also think that they are kinder than younger people. They say: "When people grow older, they start to share love."

The resentment of the elderly towards present time and young generation contains a paradox in that the elderly also value the present time and try to learn new things and, more importantly, act like younger generation, to which we now turn.

(2) Age denial and denial of oneself

While the glorification of old age separates the elderly from the rest of the society, the elderly's constant yearning for activity, associated with youthfulness and productivity, unites them with society and encompasses them within the society's larger ethos. The denial of old age assumes such forms as dissociation from the Senior Center, positive evaluation of youth, involvement with "work," and the effort to look young, all of which serve to emphasize unity with the society rather than separation from it.

Dissociation from the Senior Center appears when younger members of the Center pretend that they go to the Center mainly because they are giving a ride to someone else. These people underemphasize their eligibility of being a member of the Senior Citizen Center and overemphasize their assistance to another person by assuming a self-important role. They say that they take a relative or a friend to the Center. Outside the Senior Center, many people who are over fifty-five years old and thus eligible to be a member of an organization such as the Senior Center feel offended when asked whether they belong to a Senior Center. Objecting to the question, many people say: "I am not that old yet!"

Positive evaluation of youth appears by emphasizing the similarities more than differences between the young and old in the society. Eunice, a member of the Senior Center, has a half hour show on the local television. Although the show is about the activities of senior citizens, and contains interviews with the elderly, it is called "Never Grow Old," as if there were something wrong with growing old. A similar show on a local television in Los Angeles, California, is called "Stay Young." There seems to be many meanings associated with the terms "old" and "young" in American culture. As mentioned in the beginning of this section, asking somebody's age is taboo in American culture. Many elderly themselves do not specify their age, or they prefer to say they are 'above a certain age.'[25] Occasionally, however, some elderly openly state their age. Interestingly, many of them insist that they are, say, 69, 75, 80, or 95 years "young." During the fieldwork, I heard many people who mentioned their age that way. Some people even objected to those who used the term "old" in talking about their age.

In English, the phrase which is used to ask somebody's age encompasses the idea of oldness. The elderly seem to react against the oldness content existing in such sentences as "How **old** are you?", and "I am ... years **old**." To them, "How **old** are you" contains oldness as opposed to youth. This is more obvious when one is compared with another person in terms of age; one is either younger, older, or as old as another person. "How old are you?" in English can be contrasted with a similar sentence in other languages. In French, for instance, one asks "quel age avez-vous" which literally means "which age do you have?" In Arabic, one asks "kam sana omr-e k" which literally means "how much is your lifetime?" In Persian, one asks "chand sal darid" which literally means "how many years do you have?" To compare one's age with another, in French one is either more aged or less aged than another one. In Arabic and in Persian, one is either bigger or smaller than another person. In

Persian, when two persons are as old as each other, the term "of the same year" is used. The point is that in all the three languages mentioned above the terms "age," "lifetime," and "year" are neutral and value-free in terms of oldness and youth, whereas in English the term **old** is not.

Positive evaluation of youth is also visible in the stereotypes about oldness and the elderly. Such phrases as "old fogey," "dirty old man," "old-fashioned," "old witch," "over hill (or down hill)," and "you can't teach an old dog new tricks" express negative connotations associated with oldness. They implicitly express such ideas that an old person is out-dated; an old person is not supposed to have sexual desires; and the mind of an old persons decays. The elderly are aware of these cultural expressions. They try to stress that, in spite of old age, no difference exists between them and younger people in the society with regard to learning, activity, and productivity. One very active member of the Senior Center once suggested to the Administration that they set up a booth in the biggest shopping Mall in town in order to inform people about the Senior Center. She said:

> We [the elderly] need publicity. We should tell people
> that the activities at the Senior Center are educational,
> too. We have to show people that we do something
> more than just playing cards and bingo.

Note that this statement also symbolizes the informant's effort to prevent the peer group from "giving all of us [the elderly] a bad name."

In this category (i.e., positive evaluation of youth), one can also include the way in which the elderly appear. Appearing younger is admired in American society. Anthropologists report from some other societies in which an elderly person is frowned upon if he tries to look younger. Robert Smith (1961:95-100) writes about the elderly in Japan: "The older adult is not...a prisoner of time, nor does he feel that it is running out for him. He makes no effort to appear younger than he is." Colleen Rustom (1961:101-103) reports about the Burmese elderly woman for whom there is a "code of conduct" which is "not to look young." Rustom (Ibid.) writes that an elderly woman:

must not try to appear younger than she is, she must not beautify herself with cosmetics, elaborate hair styles, or jewelry. She should not wear 'unsuitable colors,' that is, 'the soft and tender colors' (pastels) and 'bold or bright colors'.

In the United States, on the other hand, one must try not to look old. The media communicate to the elderly that they are no longer attractive: if they are to prove themselves through being attractive, they must put on more and more make-up. The cosmetic commercials specify if their product does not show oldness and/or stops a person from aging (i.e., developing wrinkles).[26] Wearing colorful clothes and cosmetics are accepted for the elderly. So are wearing wigs (toupees) or dyeing one's hair to hide baldness or graying of the hair.

At the Senior Center, women wear colorful clothes. They are very formally dressed in larger gatherings (e.g., birthday parties). They also wear various types of jewelry: earings, necklaces, bracelets, rings, etc. It is very common for the elderly to wear jewelry appropriate to such ritually significant recurrent occasions as Christmas. They attach Christmas tree pins to their dresses, wear earings which look like bells, etc. They also wear a good amount of make-up, and are conscious of its freshness. They usually renew their lipstick after each meal. Men also wear formal clothings. In larger gatherings, they always wear a jacket and a tie. Some men wear three piece suits. Thus, there does not seem to be a distinct difference between the clothings of the elderly and those of the younger generation in American culture. In some cases, the clothings of elderly women are more elaborate than those of younger women, particularly in the case of jewelry.

Another common cliche about the elderly is that they are asexual. The elderly make a conscious effort to prove otherwise. Speaking about sex is not taboo at the Senior Center. On a board in the craftsroom, there is a white, circle shaped, handcrafted cushion on which the phrase "Sexy Senior Citizen" is inscribed with a red thread. Jokes about sex are sometimes heard at the Center. Of course, since most relationships are formal and based on the performance of a special activity, the jokes take place somewhat secretly and among those who are close to each other. Men sometimes tease widows who are taking a cruise and ask whether they are going on a "love boat" to find a husband.

The third category symbolizing the denial of aging is apparent in the elderly's involvement with "work" in the sense of performing various activities which has been mentioned in detail (see chapter IV). The elderly portray themselves as being active in many different ways. When asked what the Senior Center means to you, almost all members have a positive attitude towards it and express its meaningfulness. In responding to this question, Catherine said:

> I come to the Center as often as I can, usually two or three days a week. I am glad to get out of the house and become involved in the many activities. I have learned how to use my hands instead of holding them.

When asked whether they would still go to the Center, if there were no activities, most people did not know what to say because they could not imagine the Center with no activities. Some asked what the use of a Senior Center would be without any activities. It would be a safe guess that many people would not go to the Center if it did not offer any activities.

Some elderly believe that keeping busy stops one from getting old. As one of my informants said: "Most people say that as you get old, you have to give up things. I think you get old because you give up things." Another person said: "I'm afraid if someone tried to retire me completely I'd go crazy." One other informant said: "It is through activities that people never grow old." A ninety-eight year "young" woman, Irena, once said: "I stay young by working hard every day. I do the same amount of work that I did at fifty. I don't feel old." The same argument goes for volunteering. The elderly say that volunteering keeps one involved, interested, and "young." An elderly gentleman once told me "When I hit sixty, I felt I was dying. My solution for not feeling that way was volunteering." Thus, when he was close to retirement and losing his identity as a member of the working adult group, he began searching for a replacement. His solution was "to work without pay." The result, in many cases, is that the older person strives to be active and to overlook the inabilities he may have owing to being old. The following poem published in **the League of Older Americans** (1980:11) portrays the value placed in ignoring aging.

I'm fine

There's nothing whatever the matter with me,
I'm fine and healthy as can be;
I have arthritis in both my knees;
And when I talk I talk with a wheeze;
My pulse is weak and my blood is thin;
But I'm awfully well for the shape I'm in.
I think my liver is out of whack,
And I've a terrible pain in my back.
My hearing's poor and my eyes are dim;
Most everything seems out of my trim.
The way I stagger sure is a crime--
I'm likely to fall most any time;
But all things considered I'm feeling fine.
Now the moral is--as the tale we unfold,
That for you and me who are growing old:
It's better to say, "I'm fine" with a grin,
Than to tell everyone the shape we are in.

Anonymous

The elderly themselves reject their age. As one senior citizen said: "There is no excuse for a person not to stay young." Another person said: "We never say someone is old." In an interview in the show called "Never grow old," the interviewer asked a ninety-seven year "young" woman the reason for staying young. The interviewee answered: "I never thought I was old." The woman who was in charge of the show, herself an active member of the Senior Center, always interviewed those elderly who were very active, looked healthy compared to other elderly, could speak nicely, and could do something extraordinary. On different shows, for example, she interviewed a ninety year old man who could play banjo and sing, an elderly woman who could play the piano beautifully, a couple in a senior citizen bowling tournament, a group of senior citizens who were square dancing, another group who were dancing Hawaiian, a ninety year old woman who started learning how to paint when she was seventy years old, etc. She never interviewed those who did not do something extraordinary, who had gone through a jaw surgery (because of cancer), or a hip surgery (because of arthritis), or those who had some other unfortunate diseases.

There is often a tension among senior citizens themselves with regard to their age. At the Senior Center, for instance, some people make an effort to show that they are a number of years younger than others. This is quite visible among the "oral history" activity group. This group tries to remember certain social events. Once a person said something, and asked a woman whether she remembered it. The woman smiled sarcastically, winked and said: "No, I don't. I was a little girl, then." At one monthly birthday party at the Senior Center, a man distributed some papers and asked people to vote for a representative. He, then, mentioned that only those over sixty years of age can vote. All the people at the party smiled and said that they were less than sixty. On another occasion, I said a group of elderly that gerontologists recognize two groups of elderly: the young-old (those below seventy-five years of age), and the old-old (those above seventy-five). Many people smiled and said how nice it was that they were still "young-old."

Many senior citizens consider others old and criticize them because of their old age. A member of the Senior Center, for instance, tells everybody that she is living with an "old" woman. Once, the oral history group had gone to a school to talk about life in the past. One woman who assumed the role of chairperson (organizer) introduced all the members who were present. When she was introducing a ninety year old woman, who came to this country as an immigrant, she said: "The group has a unique person, a German woman who can tell us about life in Germany. However, she has two problems. She can't hear well and she likes to talk." The elderly criticize other elderly for being talkative. Interestingly, most of the people who criticize others are fond of talking themselves, too. On another occasion (1986) a group of senior citizens were discussing politics. One woman criticized the President of the country for being too old. She said:

> I don't like the President. He is too old. He sleeps a lot.
> He takes a lot of vacations and we taxpayers should pay
> for it. He stops working at 5:00 o'clock. He should not
> be a President. I am an old person and I am not a
> President, but I am exhausted in the evening.

As a group, the elderly present an insightful portrait of American culture. It helps one to see the central role of work as the source of individual's dignity and indeed identity. Although outside the work sphere, children take pride in their successes while preparing themselves to be "the ideal American:" well- trained, efficient, number one, and achiever. While in a similar state, i.e., outside the work sphere, the elderly are in a difficult position. The more they take themselves seriously, the less the society accepts them. At the same time they have to fight the defeating battle of aging. Formally they are excluded from the central stage of the cultural theater of American society, the work place. They create their own theater by associating themselves with activity centers (or other organizations) through which to continue their identity of what Benjamin Franklin called *homo fabor*. They establish a relationship with these centers which resembles the relationship of those in the work sphere to their place of work.

---

1 One of the findings of a nationwide survey, conducted by Harris and Associates (1981), was that the percentage of older respondents listing fear of crimes as a serious personal problem was substantial (25%) and was slightly higher than the percentage among younger people (20%). According to Belsky (1984:10) the great fear of crime among the elderly may be adaptive, "perhaps because older people are more fearful, they are more cautious to avoid high-risk situations."

2 Speech of the executive director of the Center on the 25th anniversary of the establishment of the Center. The text of this speech is in the author's possession.

3 "Words and Music" is the title of one of the humanities courses which was offered at the Center in Spring 1985.

4 The crafts activity group makes many handcrafted objects in order to be sold in the annual Bazar. It also makes a quilted blanket which is given as a prize for the lottery which is administered during the Bazaar. The term "Hawaian," in the director's speech, refers to the design of the quilted blanket in that particular year.

5 Note the usage of the term work in this statement.

6 The Center has an arrangement with one of the local motels so as to enable the members to swim there one hour each week.

7 "The Holiday Fever" is the name of a public music show (held in May 1985) to raise money for the Center. Some professionals and some members of the Senior Center volunteered their services. It generated $2500.00 for the Center.

8 At the annual dance, the entertainment includes refreshment, prizes, music, dancing and watching the acts of the organizers (as clowns, cowboys, etc.).

9 Usually during the birthday parties of the months of December and February.

10 The prizes are provided by the members of the activity group themselves and not by the Senior Center. Every month, the members of the Bingo group pay a small fee for prizes, usually handled by two members who buy prizes, and distribute them during the games.

11 About fifty players participate in each session and five to ten rouds of games are played.

[12] The "take home prizes" could be seen as a reward for the elderly for making the effort of coming to the center. One gets paid for going to the "work place," one gets a prize for going to the "Center," and playing bingo.

[13] Interestingly, the elderly see getting the prizes as an "achievement." Once, I won several times, and wanted to divide my prizes with a woman who had not won anything. She refused to accept my offer, and argued: "These are yours. **You** have won them" (original emphasis).

[14] Note the striking similarities between the instructions given to the elderly and those given to the children (e.g., behave yourselves, don't cheat, be honest).

[15] The elderly themselves, however, consider getting prizes as an "achievement" rather than pure chance.

[16] The similarities between children and the elderly are also striking as regards the institutions which exist for each of them. Parents usually leave their children with baby sitters or in day care centers to go to work or social gatherings. Baby sitters, in form of nurses (at home), and day care centers, in form of "adult day care centers," also exist for the elderly.

[17] Note the usage of the term "work" by this person.

[18] Note the usage of the term "work" here.

[19] This may be due to the fact that the Senior Center has been established to enhance the lives of the elderly and teach them to cope with aging. Death may be considered a failure.

[20] Many senior citizens do not think very highly of themselves, especially with regard to their age. The statement of this older person contains not only his age-consciousness, but also his astonishment about the younger people who "enjoy" working around the elderly.

[21] The point about "age" is worth noting from different angles. On the one hand, people try to ignore old age. It is not considered polite to ask somebody's age. This is, in a way, escaping old age. Thus, people do not know much about old age, and perhaps, do not enjoy it. Yet, people live longer and longer. On the other hand, old age is more associated with deterioration, than with growth. Those who have not seen each other for several years sometimes express astonishment or make comments on how good each looks regardless "of all those years." It is assumed that one should not look **good** as one ages. Moreover, the science of medicine is changing the meaning of age. A sixty year old person may have the kidney of a twenty year old through transplant. The question is whether the person is sixty years old, twenty, or something different.

[22] In practice, however, in order to attract more attendance, the Senior Center (and the elder's club) invite all the members to attend the activities of the club.

[23] Before the appointed day for the bazaar, the Senior Center asks the members to donate home-made pastries and other items to be sold in the bazaar. When there are not enough donations, the Center purchases pastries from public bakeries and sells them as home-made. In this case, the elderly (or the Center) take advantage of their status (being old) associated with home-made and traditional cuisine.

[24] Resentment exists towards younger generation as a whole. It is variable in the elderly's relationship with specific younger persons.

25 The resentment to mention one's age in American culture can be contrasted to that of other cultures, for example that of an Iranian villager. In the latter younger people tend to increase their age by at least ten years. This is to gain respect, since the older the person the more respected in the community.

26 Among the many products which presumably prevent aging, note television commercials on "Oil of Olay" and "Age-controlling products. The following excerpt is taken from an Estee Lauder advertisement:

> Now Estee Lauder has created the cream that encourages all skins to do what young skin does on its own. While only nature controls the aging process, **Age-Controlling Creme** actually helps increase the ability of the cells to renew themselves faster and act younger.... Used day and night, **Age-Controlling Creme** actually helps control the signs of aging-- fine lines, flakiness and wrinkles, due to dryness. The result: skin that looks smooth, soft, radiant and young. (Original emphases).

Bibliograpgy

Anderson, Nels. 1964. **Dimensions of Work: The Sociology of Work Culture.** New York: David McKay Company, Inc.

Anderson, R. And Associates. 1975. **Equality in Health Service.** Cambridge, MA: Ballinger.

--------, ----------------. 1976. **Two Decades of Health Expenditure.** Cambridge, MA: Ballinger.

Atchley, R.C. 1971. "Disengagement among professors," **Journal of Gerontology.** Volume 26 (October).

--------, ---. 1976. **The Sociology of Retirement.** New York: Schenkman.

Barnett, S. and M. Silverman. 1979. **Ideology and Everyday Life.** Ann Arbor: The University of Michigan Press.

Belsky, J. 1984. **The Psychology of Aging.** Monterey, Cal.: Brooks Cole Publishing Company.

Bengston, Vern L. 1973. **The Social Psychology of Aging.** New York: The Bobbs-Merrill Company, Inc.

Binstock, R. H. 1972. "Interest Group, Liberalism and the Politics of Aging," **Gerontologist.** 12: 265-80.

Bohannan, Paul. 1955. "Some Principles of Exchange and Investment among the Tiv," **American Anthropologist.** 57: 60-70.

Breen, L.Z. 1963. "Retirement-norms, Behaviour, and Functional Aspects of Normative Behaviour," in **Processes of Aging.** R. H. Williams *et al.* (eds). Englewood Cliffs, N.J.: Prentice-Hall.

139

Britton, J. 1958. "Assessment of Service for the Aged in Rural Communities," **Journal of Gerontology**. 13: 67-69.

Burgess, Ernest W. (ed). 1960. **Aging in Western Societies**. Chicago: The University of Chicago Press.

Bulter, Robert N. and Mary I. Lewis. 1983. **Aging and Mental Health**. New York: New American Library.

Caillois, R. 1961. **Man, Play and Games**. M. Barash (Translated). New York: The Free Press of Glencoe.

Clark, M. 1975. "Contributions of Cultural Anthropology to the study of the Aged," in **Cultural Illness and Health: Essays in Human Adaptations**. L. Nader and T.W. Maretzki (eds). Anthropological Studies. N0. 9.

Clark, M. and B.G. Anderson. 1980. **Culture and Aging: An Anthropological Study of Older Americans**. New York: Arno Press.

Corning, P. 1969. **The Evolution of Medicare from Idea to Law**. Washington D.C.

Cumming, E. M. and W. Henry. 1961. **Growing Old**. New York:Basic Books.

Dahl, G. 1972. **Work, Play, and Worship**. Minneapolis: Augsburg Publishing House.

De Grazia, S. 1962. **Of Time, Work and Leisure**. New York: Twentieth Century Fund.

De Tocqeville, A. 1835. "Democracy in America," reprinted from Dempcracy in America, in **The Character of Americans**. McGiffert (ed).

Dickenson, Paul. 1971. "Striking out on Your Own," **Washington Monthly** (August).

Dumazedier, J. 1968. "Leisure," **International Encyclopedia of Social Sciences**.

Dumont, Louis. 1968. "The Modern Conception of Individual, Notes on its Genesis," **Contribution to Indian Sociology**. Vol. III

------, ---. 1970. "Religion, Politics and Society in the Individualistic Universe," in **Proceedings of the Royal Anthropological Institute of Great Britain**.

Evans-Pritchard, E. E. 1940. **The Nuer: A Description of the Modes of Livelihood and Political Institutions of a Nilotic People**. New York: Oxford University Press.

Fischer, D. H. 1977. **Growing Old in America**. New York:

Oxford University Press.

Fowler, J. 1970. "Knowledge, need and use of services among the aged," in **Health Care Services for the Aging**. C. Osterbind (ed). Gainsville: University of Florida Press.

Friedman, E. A. 1961. "The impact of aging on the social structure," in **Handbook of Social Gerontology**. Clark Tibbitts (ed). Chicago: University of Chicago Press. pp. 120-144.

Fry, Christine L. and Contributors. 1981. **Dimensions: Aging, Culture and Health**. New York: Praeger.

---, -----------. 1980. **Aging in Culture and Society: Comparative Viewpoints and Strategies**. New York: Praeger.

Givehcian, Fatemeh. 1983. "**The Portrayal of Grandparents in American Popular Culture.**" Master's Thesis, University of Virginia.

Godelier, M. 1975. "Mode of Production, Kinship, and Demographic Structures," in **Marxist Analysis and Social Anthropology**. M. Bloch (ed). London: Malaby Press.

Gregory, C. 1981. "Kula Gift Exchange and Capitalist Commodity Exchange: A Comparison," in **Comparative and Historical Perspective on Massim Exchange**. S. Leach and E. R. Leach (ed).

Hanssen et al. 1978. "Correlates of Senior Center Participation," **Gerontologist**. 18:193-99.

Harris, D. K. and W. E. Cole. 1980. **Sociology of Aging**. Boston: Houghton Miffin Company.

Harris, L. and Associates 1975. **The Myth and Reality of Aging in America**. Washington D. C. : National Council on the Aging.

Hughes, C. C. 1961. "The Concept and use of time in the middle years: The St. Laurence Island Eskimos," in **Aging and Leisure**. R. W. Kleemeier (ed). New York: Oxford University Press.

Huyck, M. H. 1974. **Growing Older**. Englewood Cliffs, N.J.: Prentice Hall.

Inkeles, A. 1980. "Continuity and Change in the American National Character," **The Tocqeville Review**. Vol. II No. II-III: 20-51.

Johnson, D. 1971. **Idlehaven: Community Building among the Working Class Retired**. Berkeley: University of California Press.

Johnson, P. E. 1978. **A Shopkeeper's Millennium**. New York: Hill and Wang.

Kaplan Max. 1960. **Leisure in America: A Social Inquiry**. New York: John Wiley & Sons.

Kart, Cary and Barbara B. Manard. 1976. **Aging in America**. New York: Alfred Publishing Co., Inc.

Keith, J. 1980. "The best is yet to be: toward an anthropology of old age," **Annual Review of Anthropology**. pp. 339-364.

-----, -. 1982. **Old People as People: Social and Cultural Influence on Aging and Old People**. Boston: Little Brown.

Kertzer, David I. and Jennie Keith. (eds.). 1984. **Age and Anthropological Theory**. Ithaca: Cornell University Press.

Kleemeier, Robert W. (ed) 1961. **Aging and Leisure: A Research Perspective into the Meaningful use of Time**. New York: Oxford University Press.

Kluckhohn, C. 1949. **Mirror for Man**. New York: Whittlesey House.

Krout, J. A. 1983. "Correlates of Senior Center Utilitarian," **Research on Aging**. 5(3):339_352.

Larrabee, Eric and Rolf Meyeshn. (eds). 1958. **Mass Leisure**. Glencoe, Illinois: The Free Press.

Levi-Strauss, C. 1969. **Elementary Structure of Kinship**. Translated by J. H. Bell and J.R. Von Strumer. R. Needham (eds). Boston: Beacon Press.

------------, -. 1962. **The Savage Mind**. Chicago: The University Press.

------------, -. 1983. **Structural Anthropology.** Vol. 1. Translated by Jacobson and B.G. Schoepf. New York: Basic Books, Inc.

Lubove, Roy. 1968. **The Struggle for Social Security:1900-1935**. Cambridge, Ma: Harvard University Press.

Manney, J. D. Jr. 1975. **Aging in American Society: an Examination of Concepts and Issues**. Ann Arbor, MI: The University of Michigan Press.

Mathaei, J. A. 1982. **An Economic History of Women in America.** New York: Schocken Books.

Mendelson, M. A. 1975. **Tender Loving Creed**. New York: Knopf.

Moore, S. F. 1978. "Old age in a life-term Social Arena: Some Changa of Kiliminjaro in 1974," in **Life's Career-Aging:**

Cultural Variations in Growing Old. B. Myerhoff and Simic (eds). Beverly Hills: Sage. pp. 23-76.

Morgan, J. N. et al. 1964. "Productive Americans: a study of how individuals contribute to economic progress," **Survey Research Center Monograph**. No. 43. Ann Arbor:Institute for Social Research, University of Michigan Press.

Meyerhoff, B. 1979. **Number Our Days**. New York: Sutton.

The National Council of Aging. 1976. **The Indivisible Elderly**. Washington D.C.

------------------------------. 1977. **Senior Center Operation; a Guide to Organization Management**. Washington D.C.

------------------------------. 1979. **Fact Book on Aging; A Profile of America's Older Population**. Washington D.C.

------------------------------. 1980. **Senior Centers and the At-Risk Older Person**. Washington D.C.

------------------------------. 1982. **Comprehensive Service Delivery Through Senior Centers and Other Community Focal Points: a Resource Mannual**. Washington D.C.

Neugarten, Bernice L. (ed). 1968. **Middle Age and Aging. a Reader in Social Psychology**. Chicago: The University of Chicago Press.

O'Toole, J. et al. 1978. **Work in America: Report of Social Task Force to the Secretary of Health, Education and Welfare**. Cambridge, Ma: The MIT Press.

Parker, S. L. 1982. **Work and Retirement**. Boston: George Allen & Unwin.

Queen, S. A. and R. W. Habenstein. 1961. "The colonial family in North America," in **The Family in Various Cultures**. New York: J. B. Lippincott Company. 4th edition (1974), pp. 330-344

Rhee, H. A. 1974. **Human Ageing and Retirement**. Geneva: International Social Security Association.

Rowe, W. 1961. "The middle and later years in Indian society," in **Aging and Leisure**. R.W. Kleemeier (ed.). New York: Oxford University Press, pp. 104-109.

Rustom, C. 1961. "The later years of life and the use of time among the Burmans," in **Aging and Leisure**. R.W. Kleemeier (ed.). New York: Oxford University Press, pp. 100-103.

Sahlins, M. 1969. "The original affluent society," in **Man the Hunter**. Irven DeVore and Richard Lee (eds.). Chicago: Adline

Pub. Co.

Salz, B. 1955. "The human element in Industrialization," **Economic Development and Cultural Change**. Vol. IV, No. 1, Pt. 2 (Special supplement).

Sapir, D. J. and C. J. Crocker. 1977. **The Social Use of Metaphor: Essays on the Anthropology of Rhetoric**. Philadelphia: The University of Pennsylvania Press.

Sarason, Seymour B. 1977. **Work, Aging and Social Change: Professionals and the One-Life Career Imperative**. New York: The Free Press.

Schneider, D. M. 1968. **American Kinship: A Cultural Account**. 2nd edition (1980). Chicago: The University of Chicago Press.

Schramm, W. and R. Storey. 1961. **Little House: A Study of Senior Citizens**. Menlo Park, Cal: Peninsula Volunteers, Inc.

Shanas, Ethel. *et al.* **Old People in Three Industrial Societies**. New York: Atherton Press.

Simmons, L. 1945. **The Role of the Aged in Primitive Society**. New Haven: Yale University Press.

Skidmore, M. 1970. **Medicare and the American Rhetoric of Reconciliation**. University, Al: The University of Alabama Press.

Smith, Bert K. 1973. **Aging in America**. Boston: Beacon Press.

Smith, R. J. 1961. "Japan: the later years of life and the concept of time," in **Aging and Leisure**. R.W. Kleemeier (ed.). New York: Oxford University Press.

Strumpel, B. (ed.). 1976. **Economic Means for Human Needs: Social Indicators of Well-Being and Discontent**. Ann Arbor: Survey Research Centers Institute for Social Research, the University of Michigan Press.

Terkel, Studs. 1972. **Working: People Talk about What They Do all Day and How they Feel about What They Do**. New York: Pantheon Books.

Tibbitts, Clark. (ed.). 1960. **Handbook of Social Gerontology: Social Aspects of Aging**. Chicago: The University of Chicago Press.

Tonnies, Ferdinand. 1957. **Community and Society: (Gemeinschaft and Gesellschaft)**. Trans. Charles P. Lomis. East Lansing, MI: The Michigan State University Press.

Tuckman, J. 1967. "Factors related to attendance in a center for older people," **Journal of the American Geriatrics Society.** 14: 474-479.

Turner, Victor. 1978. "Comments and Conclusions," in **The Reversible World.** B. Babcock (ed.). Ithaca: Cornell University Press, pp. 276-296.

Twain, Mark. 1876. **The Adventures of Tom Sawyer.** Chicago: The American Publishing Company.

Vogt, E.Z. 1955. **Modern Homesteaders: The Life of a Twentieth Century Frontier Community.** Cambridge: The Belknap Press.

Wallace, A. 1980. **Rockdale.** New York: W.W. Norton and Company.

Warner, W. L. 1953. **American Life: Dream and Reality.** Chicago: The University Press.

Weber, Max. 1958. **The Protestant Ethic and the Spirit of Capitalism.** New York: Charles Scribner's Sons.

Wilensky, Harold. 1966. "Work as a social problem," in **Social Problems: a Modern Approach.** Howard S. Becker. (ed). New York: Wiley.

Wilson, M. 1951. **Good Company: a Study of Nyakyusa Age Villages.** New York: Oxford University Press.

Winick, Charles. 1964. "Atonie: the psychology of the unemployed and the marginal worker," in **The Frontiers of Management Psychology.** George Fish. (ed). New York: Harper and Row.